POETRY

Nina Cassian   Carmen Firan

INTERVIEWS AND ENCOUNTERS

CONVERSATIONS

The Sheep Meadow Press
Rhinebeck, NY

Designed and typeset by The Sheep Meadow Press
Distributed by The University Press of New England

All inquiries and permission requests should be addressed to the publisher:
The Sheep Meadow Press
PO Box 84
Rhinebeck, NY 12572

Library of Congress Cataloging-in-Publication Data

Cassian, Nina, author.
[Poems. Selections. English]
Interviews and encounters : poetry and conversation between Nina Cassian and
Carmen Firan.
pages cm
ISBN 978-1-937679-40-8
I. Firan, Carmen, author. II. Title.
PC840.13.A9A2 2015
859'.134--dc23

ACKNOWLEDGMENTS

All our gratitude to Stanley Moss for making possible the publication of this book.

Carmen Firan & Maurice Edwards

Grateful acknowledgment also to the translators and publishers for granting to the Estate of Nina Cassian, and to Carmen Firan, permission to reproduce the poems in this volume. Special thanks to W. W. Norton. Co.

Nina Cassian's "Last Poems" were previously published in the *American Poetry Review*.

CONTENTS

Poems by Nina Cassian

Poems by Carmen Firan

*Translators' names appear after their translations

PREFACE

THE KINGDOM OF GODDESSES
by Andrei Codrescu

Once upon a time, which is the future, there was, is, and will be a land ruled by women poets. In this land, which is not in the least imaginary, but, on the contrary, is ultrarealistic and lucid, there is a park where two goddesses held a colloquium. The duo of Nina Cassian and Carmen Firan, also known as the Wind and the Sea, talked about life, love, poetry, death, and the conditions that made the 20th century a crossroads for humanity. I kid you not: this is what they talked about, with candor, probity, and courage. In support of their conversation they also collected some of their best work and bracketed their dialogue with the unarguable substance of their poetries.

"Dialogue of the Wind and Sea" is a complex wilderness, an ecosystem of similarities and differences. The similarities are graspable: both Nina Cassian and Carmen Firan have dedicated themselves to poetry above all else. Both of them were born in Romania in the 20th century. Both were participants and actors in the tumultuous history of their country. Their sensibilities were formed in the language of their birth, and educated by the reading of the best of their national literature. Circumstances forced both out of their native country. Both of them started writing in English later in life, with some difficulty, but with absolute fidelity to poetry. Both are urban to the core, inhabitants of great cities, Bucharest and New York. And both of them are women who have made of their femininity a weapon and a fan. If one were to draw this object it would be by an exquisitely painted Japanese fan that could suddenly turn its gentle blades into stilettoes. Each of them lived several lives. They were friends.

The differences are as striking. Nina Cassian was already celebrated in Romania long before Carmen Firan was born. She started writing young under the waning but still powerful black sun of the Romanian avant-garde. In the barbed-wire Soviet years that followed the war she made her peace with communism, a system of belief and ideas that she never renounced. She resolved the chasm between those ideas, and their perversion by the rigid and murderous authoritarianism that followed, by producing a body of work acceptable to the regime, and maintaining her self-respect by writing children's books. She composed music and invented a musical language. Prodded by the younger woman, who despises the communists with a passion, Cassian regrets her "self-mutilating" efforts and her "fatal hiatuses" of years when she renounced both poetry and music. Her faith in the communist ideal and her refusal of any kind of religious or spiritual palliatives are firmly opposed to Carmen Firan's spiritual quest and respect for traditional beliefs. Their dialogue on these matters is tough and without qualifiers. Such firm opposition would have made enemies of men: yet the two stay friends because history and ideas are secondary to the facts of their womanhood and their art. Listening to the rich, and often rough conversation one hears biographical confidences and stubbornly held ideas. The effect is voyeuristic and delicious. Several times, Nina asks Carmen to turn off the recorder, to speak off the record. Carmen doesn't, and it's a good thing. We are gratified by the depth and strength of what follows. We understand also that many of their conversations, as is the case between friends, will never be known. And, amazingly, they engage also in a long poetic collaboration, giving of their selves in the way only their art can.

Carmen Firan, though much younger, loves the older poet's work, and is enthusiastically encouraging her to keep writing in Romanian, and to have no fear of the English language. Carmen has written in both languages, and her body of work is diverse: poetry, reportage, fiction. She is also a muse and a benefactor to Romanian poets who, like her, have made the huge transcontinental leap between cultures and languages. Her poetry, both in translation and in English, seeks the sublime but is roughly cognizant of reality's hard edges. Ironically, the spiritual journey in her writing is akin to Cassian's early idealistic impulse, though politically inimical. Cassian's poetry finds carnal joy and sorrow in the present moment, while Firan is often tuned in to something ineffable.

Nina Cassian died as she had lived: courageously, and without fuss. Her last love and husband, Maurice Edwards, a musician himself, made a selection of her work that is supremely loving and good. His musical ear resonated to her rhythms. Nina had a charmed life and good luck. She was loved and her rare talent was recognized. Carmen Firan has collected a formidable body of her own poetry too, much of it translated by first-rate American poets, who recognize its unique quality. Both women are essential to something in the passage between the 20th and the 21st century: the miracle of joining hugely different worlds through the language of poetry. They were fated to meet and make this book. Nina would have scoffed at the word "fate," but would have expressed the same sentiment with a synonym, and loved the result.

Oz, May 26, 2015

Last Poems

by Nina Cassian

composed in English
or translated by Nina Cassian

Adieu

Adieu again, my smile-less summer,
adieu to me, as well, the inconsolable.
From everything I've tasted, what's left is just
the complicit stone of memory
upon my deeply buried body.

Don't write my name on the slab,
I'm fed up with inscriptions, with my skin,
with the branch of my blood, with poetry.

There won't be any Second Coming.

It's a Pity

It's a pity, and I'm truly sorry that I won't reach the solemn hour
    dressed in the clear outfit of Spirit.
Fog surrounds my Present and plunges me into a Nothingness,
    exempt of grandeur.
Oh, I wish I could have uttered the Syllable and the High Sound
    that could pierce the Fish's ear
    and startle the White Owl in her sleep.
I wish I could have drawn a Last Will in the air with my right hand,
    and could close my eyes willingly on a last loving glance.

There is fog. I cannot see. I cannot talk.
The world turns its back on me.

Transfiguration

I am obliged to believe that it's true—
this mystical fog over the ocean,
and the endless shore waves, and me—as if from Atlantis!

Far out there, a few people are taking a sunbath
on the shore of another sea
to which I was once related through blood
and love's seed.

Here the sand is brutal, and a strange cold
turns my age blue.
My skin is streaked red and white:
I am a striped flag—occidental.

The Last Flag

I'm ashamed of my widowhood
because everybody treats me so nicely
and I don't reward them as they deserve.
I'm ashamed of my absolute loneliness,
and my last flag floats
over the last rampart like a rhyme,

although I want to die in free verse.

The Sun's Missing Shadow

This sun does not leave a shadow,
nor even a trace on my discolored body.
I remain cold and intact,
like a decorative sculpture in a natural environment.

Thanks to the Maestro,
the world's eye is still contemplating me—
so do you, my airy, ethereal lover.

Recently Discovered Poems

by Nina Cassian

translated by Nina Cassian

I Cried Just Once

I cried just once in a far away Christmas,
dominated by painful old melodies—
we became their distinctive sounds,
while you, my love, were pulsating
on the invisible side of the moon,
and I in today's ongoing holiday.

And the more the holiday progressed,
your absence made my movements heavier,
until I fell down amidst the dancing creatures,
my body becoming massive and inert,
because emptied of soul.

Refusal

You offered me the beautiful apple
(I don't like apples).
You insisted, took a bite;
You spat it out and stuffed it in my mouth:
"Isn't it great?
Extend your pleasure palate,
train your tongue
with new aromas and delights.
The apple is a marvel!"
"I don't like apples," I grumbled,
My mouth filled with the apple
And my voice filled with hate:
"I let the Tree of Conscience grow!"

Purity

Amazing solitude.
Only me and my cigarette
and this tiny dragon fly
painted in Voronetz blue.

Nothing threatens me,
not even the sun.
The sky is an immense cloud
made of mother-of-pearl.
The lake is an immense cloud
of nacreous iridescence.

I am the mermaid of the lake.
I am an infinite melody,
her murmur in the rain.

And I am clean
like the poem I'm writing.

Nocturnal Moment

I am made of silence and viscera.
The green effluence of alcohol
Makes my blood phosphorescent.
By night, all felonies take place.
The law is powerless.

Tempus Fugit

Since I cannot resuscitate my first kiss,
who cares on what street it took place?

Who cares about the name of the lawn where you made love to me,
if those embraces have deserted my body?

And if these words mean something, if they have any virtue,
who cares where they were written, and that I wrote them?

If

If I had the power to give up the surrendering between the yellow corners of my bed;
if I had the power to be lulled by the false quietude of day coming to an end;
    and the seeming protection of sleep;

if I had the power not to be overtaken by surprise at this morning's fresh bread;
    or the fresh joke heard during the break at last night's meeting;

if I had the power not to be entranced by
    the voices of my friends,

when all I have to do is to shred the remains of my childhood dress,
    the blouse of my adolescence, and the bridal veil I never wore,

and to become free --

free and hopeless.

See How I Limp through the World

See how I limp through the world:
humped over and smelling
—a poor old woman.
The Doorman salutes me respectfully:
"How are you?"
"You don't want to know," I answer.
The Elevator is swallowing me.
I observe myself entering my apartment.
I flop onto my sofa.
I smell my left armpit.
I gulp down a tablet of cyanide.
I become inorganic.

The Tempest

Here, finally, is the furious Aegean:
foaming at its mouth,
dark circles under its eyes,
shouting loud battle cries at us.
Chasing the sun
the crescent flag shakes in the wind,
Ulysses doesn't dare to come home
(Penelope weaves stupidly on…).
At the border between two continents,
my lover and I test the sea with our fingers,
then withdraw them quickly,
so as not to be swallowed
by the voracious waters.

We leave the site,
and isolate ourselves
between the sheets of the hotel bed.

Untitled

I get tired.
Too many haunted sleepless nights.
Too many thin, brush-painted smiles.
I saw them at the office:
The same unflappable features.
It was them.
Them, again.
Ice. Terror.
Young and ferocious.
Them again, the bosses.
Me again, the underling.
And then they told me:
"Recite a poem for us."
Which I did.
They went on ordering my sleep
my sleeplessness
my smile, my grimace.
In the geometry of their features,
I recognize everything I hate:
the perpendicular of the guillotine,
the bisection, the being cut in two,
the obtuse angle
and the like triangles of lie.

They were just some of them…
But who was I?

DIALOGUE OF THE WIND AND SEA

by

Nina Cassian and Carmen Firan

Two Elements at Play

CARMEN FIRAN: We should find a title for our conversation, shouldn't we?

NINA CASSIAN: Let's call it *Dialogue of the Wind and the Sea*, which is the title of one of my books of poems. Who is going to be the sea?

CF: You should be.

NC: There we go.

CF: It's a game. I know you like to play.

NC: Yes, I always liked to play. The chosen ones need to play, like children. *The Glass Bead Game.* Play is both an instinct and a necessity. It calls for candor, innocence, fantasy. From play comes an appetite for poetry, for words. Then, when the vocation of poetry takes root, it brings along a certain degree of responsibility. A goal, a message for writing takes shape, but without diminishing the pleasures of play. Oh, did the surrealists know how to play!

CF: All play requires serious-mindedness and humor, even absurd games, or logical ones.

NC: Of course. Mathematics and music are games, too. Speaking of which, I used to be good at solving quadratic equations. Why am I telling this to you, a math teacher?! We're going to look like two very mischievous elements, but do we care? I don't. Let's not forget our sense of humor.

CF: Do animals have a sense of humor?

NC: I think it's humor that sets humans apart from animals. Animals do not laugh or cry. But they play. They have emotions that rise out of instincts. Yet the grin of the tiger is not a laugh. And the cry of the dog is a mere yelp. Our very human humor lets us be ironic, sarcastic, intriguing, self-deprecating. We can cry with laughter. We can peek at ourselves from outside our own selves.

CF: Is that a mask our soul puts on our face?

NC: Exactly, like you said.

CF: What about the soul then?

NC: What about it?

CF: Where is the soul located?

NC: I don't know. In the heart?

CF: I think it's everywhere.

NC: Fine. The soul is not my strong point.

CF: Do we go on playing in our sleep?

NC: Our subconscious mind is freer than we are and is better than we are at playing.

CF: Were there years when you were not up to playing?

NC: There was a time when I played less than usual, when I was called a "cerebral poet" because I had escaped the bounds of basic vocabulary. That was followed by a ludic period. My poetry has always been tidal, a back-and-forth, a continuous motion. I never wanted to lose myself in routine, so I changed my work regime often.

CF: Is there an instance of suspended, or interrupted, play in your life?

NC: I did not play under the ProletKult yoke, between 1948 and 1957. I was prisoner to an error handed down from above—a historical error I participated in, with no excuses. The damage went beyond those nine years, and it eroded my aesthetic values, but not my beliefs as an artist.

CF: There are situations in which you have to play in secret, on the sly, if only to protect your integrity or the health of your soul. At other times, you pretend to play in order to save words from emptiness and vice. Play can be freeing, but also protective, therapeutic.

NC: Yes, I have encountered play in such forms as well.

CF: The ProletKult period generated false writers and altered the work of many talented artists. Did it affect your poetry?

NC: Certainly. But I did not lose my humor, even then. I took refuge in music, in poems for children, in my own "Spargan" language—a healing invention.

CF: What are the most surprising things that happened to you?

NC: Unexpected—indeed, a mallet to the head!—was the publication in the Communist party organ, *Scânteia*, of three successive columns tearing down my debut volume, *On a Scale of 1/1*. The attack came on the heels of the abominable, notorious piece, "The Poetry of Putrefaction and the Putrefaction of Poetry," which vilified Tudor Arghezi [an esteemed major Romanian poet of the generation between the two World Wars]. The subsequent attack on me—a mere youngster who had just published her debut volume—marked out the precise height difference between the elephant and the mouse. This was the beginning of what we in Romania now call "the obsessive decade," which came with mandatory themes, a ban on metaphors, imprisonment inside an impoverished vocabulary which was supposedly "accessible to the People." For years after that, I continued to be accused of "formalism" and "decadence," despite all my self-mutilating efforts—which, luckily, did not prove to be truly self-destructive in the long term.

Also entirely unexpected was, 40 years later, the impact that my poetry had in the English-language world, not only through the books I published, but also, and especially, through international poetry festivals in Toronto, London, Rotterdam, Jerusalem, Ireland, Italy, Sweden, etc. The impact I had in the American poetry world is inexplicable for me, since most of the poetry published here is so different from mine. Perhaps this is an explanation in itself.

CF: If you could change something in your life, what would you change? And where would you start?

NC: I would not submit to the terror of Party "commissars" and write so many conventional poems of no value, as I did between 1948 and 1956. It's true that, during that ignominious period, I found refuge in composing music (an art much harder for the authorities to control) and in writing fairy tales like *Nica fara frica* (*Fearless Nica*)—a realm where metaphors or escapes into fantasy were still tolerated. But in 1957, when I finished my last composition for piano, *7 Caprices*, poetry returned to me with a vengeance, so I abandoned music for 17 years and began to write frenetically one volume after another. I came back to music in 1974, when I composed a series of pieces which, I think, are of some importance (*Vivarium, Variatio Perpetua, Tonal Fascinations*, etc.). But I really should not have abandoned music for such a long time—like I did, once again, after my exile, for another 20 years! These fatal hiatuses, which could have been avoided, would change my life!

CF: Some Romanians seem to dwell on that somber period in your life and continue to judge you today. Others have elected to linger on the paramours in your biography, which became the object of speculation in several publications and, more recently, online. Are you bothered by partial or unfair judgment?

NC: I used to be bothered by it, but no longer am. You just brought up the soul, the heart, the mind, whatever we've got inside. We each get the mind and the understanding we deserve. I enjoyed the admiration of talented and generous humans, but I also had to endure much pettiness from others. I will not say that the latter group are mediocre or frustrated. But we each have our limits and expectations, and these are either met or frustrated. I was never afraid to frustrate expectations, or to contradict them.

IDENTITY. EXILE. INTEGRATION. FAILURE.

CF: The exile's loss of identity is often invoked. Do you feel this? Is a writer exiled in a foreign language, in an alien system, fair prey for failure? When does that happen, and why? There is a transplant shock for fully formed writers who are successful in their native culture and emigrate at a certain age into an alien culture and a new language. What are the traps, the dangers awaiting them? Let's talk about your case.

NC: When I emigrated here, I was sure I would remain anonymous for the rest of my life. I was at peace with that. All I was interested in was to continue to write in Romanian and, if possible, to publish in Romanian. But when I came here, Ceaușescu was still in power—and stayed in power for another four years. So I didn't have the option of retiring or publishing in Romania. But that wasn't what affected me most. My main problem was physical survival. Suicide followed me like a guardian angel. I could end it all myself any time. What happened to me under these circumstances is actually a miracle, by which I mean something completely undeserved. I did not lift a finger. Rather, things started to fall into my lap.

CF: The luck of the Sagittarius?

NC: Perhaps, if you say that Sagittarians are said to be lucky. I had abandoned any thought of continuing my career or of finding myself in another language. I had given that up altogether.

CF: So you had come to New York with the idea of continuing to write and publish in Romania.

NC: Yes, if that was going to be possible any time soon. I did not feel like exile meant losing my status as a writer. I remained faithful to the Romanian language, which runs though my veins.

CF: Did you continue to write in Romanian from New York?

NC: When I felt like it, yes. I do not plan when to be creative.

CF: Another poet once told me she woke up each morning at five to write— either poetry or journal entries.

NC: Well may she prosper!

CF: She's no longer among us.

NC: Well, sorry. I was never disciplined like that. It was never about a poem a day for me. I wrote every time I had something to say—at any time of day, anywhere, on any piece of paper. Could I have written more? Maybe. But I never programmed my life by quantity.

CF: What about now? How much do you write?

NC: A lot less. You can see for yourself what deep old age is like. It disappoints me. I don't want to scare you, but there is no joy in it. I read, I translate, sometimes I even write, but mostly at Maurice's encouragement. It's a time for anthologies, new editions, though I fail to see the point of these things. I already said what I had to say. It was a good idea to publish my memoirs a while ago. Now I'm beginning to shed my own self. I recently donated my manuscripts, music sheets, and letters to the New York University Archives.

CF: Did your poetry change after you emigrated?

NC: No. Not until I started to write in English, which happened only after ten years, when the new language began to come naturally to me through poetry. I did not seek it myself. I had no ambition to write in English. When it came to me—I don't know what to call it, all these words are so pretentious: the muse, inspiration, whatever — it was a natural happening. These phantoms don't exist in reality.

CF: What does exist in reality then?

NC: There are outside impulses, temptations, bait. I don't know who, but someone whispers the lines to me.

CF: Aren't all these synonyms for inspiration?

NC: If you really want to call it that. But the word is so bombastic, I'm embarrassed to use it.

CF: When you started writing in English, did poetry come to you simply as dictation?

NC: Yes, I began to think and even feel in English. That's when my poetry changed. I don't know if it changed for the better or for worse. But it was a change of voice not unlike what adolescent boys experience. It was different.

CF: I know you found US editors soon after you arrived here.

NC: Far too soon—for my expectations, anyway.

CF: Were they more attracted to your older poems translated from Romanian or to the new ones written directly in English?

NC: I think they latched on to my older poems, though to my great surprise an important critic from Houston, Texas, reviewed my English-language volume and said that the book made him revise his prior conviction that poets can only write in their native tongue. He felt that the poems were natural, that they were not artificial transplants.

CF: Do you think that had to do with Maurice coming into your life, with the fact that you started speaking English at home?

NC: I think that, too, helped, to an extent, though we met late, much later. Doubtlessly, though, his presence and our communication helped. I still ask for his feedback when I write. I make mistakes sometimes—not just spelling mistakes, wording, idiom, too. I'd be lying if I said I feel totally at home in the English language.

Now I'm working on a new book of older poems in my own translation and new poems written directly in English—depending on how I feel. How does it work for you?

CF: I only started writing in English recently. About ten years after I came here, as well. A short play, essays, a film script. I translated some of my own poems, too—it's just that I'm not sure they came out the same. I added, subtracted, changed things. They're practically new poems, a whole, different thing. A language is so much more that the sum of its words. There is an energy to each language that's hard to transpose. A wonderful writer and dear friend, Bruce Benderson...

NC: ...Who wrote a great book...

CF: You must be referring to his novel *The Romanian*. Alas, Bruce tells me that I have the misfortune of speaking Romanian with my husband, Adrian. Still, we argue in English, no idea why. Perhaps because we're trying to avoid escalation: English is more somber, it has that Anglo-Saxon rigor. I think subconsciously we are trying to protect each other, because words have greater force in our native tongue.

NC: I would have preferred Maurice to be Romanian. Just for my soul. Regardless of consequences, regardless of whether it helps with literature or not.

CF: Bruce puts pressure on us to write directly in English, with all those instances of foreign writers—French, Germans, Israelis—who managed to make the leap to writing in English. His argument is that the road from finishing a book to publishing it would be a lot shorter and easier if we could short-circuit the complex and lengthy translation process. Writers are obsessed with translation and editing. And there is also the issue of quality: a translation can undermine your chances of publication. Other immigrant artists—musicians, painters—have it easier. Well, as easy as it can be in a world with different rules, with a different market terrain. But we work with words and live off of words, and we are very vulnerable to cultural differences. I know terrifying examples of writers who believe that exile brought along failure, that talent abandoned them for good, and invoke a language handicap as a main reason for this. Others explain their failure to penetrate the US publishing market by saying that they come from a minor culture, from a language of limited circulation. For others yet, inspiration took leave of them as soon as they had to cope with the practicalities of settling in a new world and to start again from scratch.

NC: It seems to me that all that is only partially grounded in reality... Before my first book was published here—which happened very quickly, only a year after I landed in New York—a writer friend kept calling me on the phone with relentless pieces of advice: "There's a formula here, and I will apply this to the novel I'm writing: sex, violence, some kind of murder..."

CF: That was before *The Da Vinci Code* and Mel Gibson's *The Passion of the Christ*—otherwise he would have added religion to the formula.

NC: Precisely. And the recipe did not work for the writer, whose name I don't want to mention, who so far has published only one, lone, awful book. The same with a novelist from the other coast, who mastered every recipe yet hasn't published one good book to date. But at least that one found a niche by exploiting sensationalism. He never made it among well-regarded writers, like Norman Manea. Manea does not write in English, yet he is the most published and awarded among the Romanian emigré writers.

CF: I know that some Romanian writers in New York and elsewhere gripe about the superficiality of American culture, and deplore the fact that the English language cannot capture "the spiritual wealth and unique feel" of our native tongue. This lament is debatable, if you ask me. But I used to hear this kind of discourse a lot in the old days, when I worked for the Romanian Cultural Institute. Mostly excuses, defensive superiority complexes. Such writers explain away their failure or, let's say, lack of recognition here in the US, by pointing to inaccurate renditions of a kind of writing whose true value is beyond the understanding of spiritually impoverished natives. But you explained very well something that I fully agree with: language is not, cannot be, a barrier. Perhaps an inability to adapt can be a barrier. You can go on being Romanian, as long as you maintain your intelligence and access to universality. But when you identify enemies in the English language, in the intellectual capacity of American editors, in "unfair" competition, or in the market need for a recipe, you fence yourself in as a writer. You end up thinking that you're always supposed to do something else than your instinct tells you to do.

NC: Beware of these pressures. Keep on being yourself, like Conrad or Nabokov. Neither *Lolita* nor *Pale Fire*, both of which are jewels, appear to have been written under the pressures of adoptive cultures. Of course, entering a new language, whatever that language may be, is the most difficult and fascinating adventure for anyone—because beyond the words themselves lay a store of history, mentality, and psychology. Language is a storage device, an instrument so complex that an encounter with a new language often means a re-making or forging or substituting one's self for another culture. That is not impossible…

CF: But is it necessary?

NC: I don't know. I am wondering myself if it's truly necessary. But I believe that you need to follow your literary destiny under any circumstances. "Stay the same, my heaven."

CF: Do emigré writers live under the specter of failure?

NC: Failure is a terrible thing. It happens to the best of us. I can give names, but it's pointless to list who made it and who didn't make it in America. Failure, like success, comes from within. If you lose your confidence, your trust in yourself, in your vocation, you fail. Once when talking to Paul Celan, who was already in Paris, I said of a common friend: "He failed." Paul jumped up: "How can you say something like that?! As long as he's alive, you can't use the word, you can't condemn him to death. You never know, he may come back."

CF: Failure doesn't take hold until you're done saying what you can say and close your eyes for good. Is that how you'd describe it?

NC: Failure is a loss of appetite. I, for instance, failed in music here in America. Even though it's supposed to be a universal language, music just left me. I lost my appetite for musical composition. I composed only one piece for piano, I have it here—it's called *Five Fingers Times Two*. It's semi-didactical, nothing more. I don't know how it all happened, maybe I got too lazy, but that for me is an unhealed wound, a permanent sore spot. Yes, I failed in music, here.

CF: I talked to many writers who came here from other East European countries. They keep coming back to the idea of failure, which tortures us, no matter how hard we try to ignore it or dress it up. I keep hearing that here the rigors of surviving are more draconian than in our countries of origin. Many had recognition at home: awards, fellowships, royalties. Once they entered into the American system, their muse was castrated, in a manner of speaking. This applies to many writers we regard with some pity and distance, saying: they had one or two or three great books "at home" but haven't done much "here." What do you think they are missing here? Flexibility, discipline, connections, luck, ambition?

NC : I don't know, to each his own. But I do think ambition can sometimes be a stimulant and sometimes an obstacle. It's of some use to have ambition in a specific project, where you have a concrete goal ahead, but, in the long run and on its own, ambition is all-devouring.

CF: Agreed. Ambition can mobilize, but can also impose subconscious limits. Moreover, people ruled by ambition are perceived as tense, spasmodic, humorless, at times opportunistic, end-justifies-the-means types. Unpleasant, even when intelligent or knowledgeable. The teacher's pet is never admired or praised, even when everybody recognizes his achievements. Are you ambitious?

NC: No. Never had any ambition for myself. I came here with no claims, no hopes of ever continuing my career.

CF: So you're the perfect object of envy: no ambition, tons of luck. That's the most irritating combination.

NC: What happened to me is indeed astonishing. But then I never put down my pencil. I never used a computer for writing—I'd write on scraps of paper, with a dull pen, in airports, on the beach, wherever I felt like writing. It's always been about lightness and spontaneity, after all.

CF: Do you think you could be accused that you were afforded the luxury of writing and doing what you wanted at a time when, in Romania, others didn't have that option? There are those grumbling voices which are not comfortable with that *dolce far niente* of your early years.

NC: Let them grumble. I've been hard of hearing for a few years now anyway. Yes, writers were privileged in Romania, it's true. But there was no luxury in that. We could go to the writers' retreats in the mountains at Sinaia, at the seaside, at the Mogosoaia palace near Bucharest, or to the restaurant of the Writers' Union at a discount. I preferred the seaside hamlet of 2 Mai; I adored the sea. There was a kind of counter-culture there. But myths are still born, fictions continue to be spun.

CF: What about in America?

NC: I came here with no survival skills: what was I to do, wait on tables or be a receptionist? I'm clumsy to the point of slapstick. All I knew were my poor little lines of poetry and some classical music. Here, composers and writers usually teach, they make a living that way. I managed to teach a bit at New York University, and I also gave piano lessons. I never had money, but then I have always been content with what I had.

CF: Do you feel spoiled by destiny?

NC: And how exactly would you define destiny?

CF: Perhaps the sum of our choices?

NC: Fine, but when you choose freedom it's one thing, and when you're forced to choose it, it's another.

CF: Did you ever have to choose something you did not want?

NC: Staying in America, for one thing. I was forced to do that.

CF: In the end, that proved to be a beneficial forced choice.

NC: That's also true.

CF: When I arrived in New York, your poetry was plastered in the subways. I got to see you reciting your poetry to sold-out audiences, seducing your readers, being fêted by the Poetry Society of America at the National Arts Club on your 80th birthday…

NC: You spoke about me at that thing…

CF: Yes, and the room was filled with the literary elite: editors at Norton and *The New Yorker*, publishers, important American writers and journalists…

and for the first time I realized that you had more recognition in the US than in our native country.

NC: But who is a prophet in his own country?! I'm interested in something else about you: Do you have regrets, older or more recent?

CF: I do have regrets, most of them healed, like old wounds. For instance, I regret I never showed my mother, who passed away too early, the tenderness I felt for her. I presumed that it was self-evident. Especially when I was young, I avoided externalizing my feelings, I felt embarrassed to declare my love or admiration for anyone, including, or perhaps especially, my parents. I was afraid of tenderness, of emotion. I had been declared rational, cerebral, ironic, and I embraced that with all the vanity of my youth.

NC: We're alike in that, too.

CF: I still regret that I did not come to this country earlier. And I regret all the days, weeks, and months I spent on false projects. I feel particularly guilty when I waste or misuse my time—on the wrong things or the wrong people, though I make course corrections as I go along. I try to do only what I really want to do and to see only people I have something to learn from. I try to say "yes" less often and to rid my nature of the kind of politeness that makes me get involved when I shouldn't. I feel good here, with my friends and family.

NC: I think you're one of those lucky Sagittarians. Also one of the harder-working ones.

CF: You were in Romania a few years ago to launch your memoirs. You did a television interview.

NC: Yes, and the first question went something like this: Don't you think that your success in America can be attributed to your being Jewish?

CF: And did you confirm that? I would have told them: "Oh yeah."

NC: Maybe I should have. I was stupefied at first. Then I answered with a joke: "An American and a Soviet journalists are in a bar. The American says to the Soviet, 'I hear there's Antisemitism in your country.' The Soviet journalist replies, 'No way! Two deputy ministers of culture are Jewish, three Moscow districts have Jewish mayors, then there are two in Leningrad, and two in the Ministry of Commerce... How many have you got?' The American goes, 'I don't know. We don't count them.'"

CF: This joke brings me to the issue of Jewish writers of some success. Where we come from, if you enjoy some measure of success, you end up being suspected: you must be Jewish, there can't be any other explanation for your success. Of course, this kind of primitive thinking runs only in some circles. I don't want to generalize. But do you think there is a Jewish issue at play in your story?

NC: After my visit to Romania, I sent a letter to a magazine in Israel in which I detailed my trip and the interview I just mentioned. As I said then, for me the "Jewish issue" only manifested itself in 1940, when I was excluded from Romanian schools. That's when I really felt it. Of course, Jews experienced the war more acutely than any other group. I knew that what was happening to this equally chosen and oppressed nation at the time was grave and laden with meaning. But what attracted me to so-called Communism—we can't even utter the word without swallowing our tongues these days—was not the situation of the Jews, but, rather, a utopian catechism of general ideas abolishing all contradictions, all bloody antagonisms among classes, races, ethnicity, or nations. It was, naturally, utopian, but it promised the abolition of the state, of money, "the devil's eye." Those were my preoccupations at the time, and I was magnetically attracted to these utopian ideals without having read up on them much. I never really read Marx, I never really read Engels—just the little brochure with the *Manifesto of the Communist Party*.

CF: Did you find any of these general ideas, as you call them, in Romanian Communism—or elsewhere?

NC: God forbid, no! I said this repeatedly: Communism never existed.

CF: Well, it did, and how! Crimes were committed in its name, generations were destroyed.

NC: No, it existed only in name, demagogically. Victims fell in its name, but then thou shalt not take names in vain…Bloody dictatorships, horrors, mass killings all happened in the name of all those generous ideas.

CF: Tell me, you say that Communism is a utopia….

NC: Oh yes.

CF: How can a utopia have concrete manifestations?

NC: It cannot! But it helped me round off my moral profile.

CF: What kind of moral profile?

NC: My total disinterest in material goods, a certain global humanitarian sensibility that protected me from arrogance and narcissism.

CF: You could have reached all that in other ways. I don't think you need to embrace Communist ideas to become a humanitarian. Besides, the Communist system proved to be inhuman.

NC: So-called Communist! I can't use the word without feeling that it's a lie, a sacrilege. It helped me rid myself of the kind of acerbic, fulminating egotism that is perhaps inherent in anyone who is creative. It did me good. Because I believed in a certain kind of harmony—however abstract and impossible it may have been—I was spared from pettiness, on a personal level.

So the "Jewish question" was never the principal motor behind my embrace of the Communist utopia. The universal embrace of all inhabitants of this Earth seemed much more important to me.

CF: Another utopia….

NC: Yes!

CF: That's where we differ. These subjects frustrate, suffocate, infuriate me.

NC: That's your problem.

CF: I return to the moment when your utopia was installed as a regime.

NC: No utopia was ever installed. It was mocked, negated, from A to Z.

CF: Then what was that thing in Romania after the War if not Communism? Was it *Alpinism*? What do you want to call that long, bloody, absurd night that fell over the country?

NC: I like Alpinism. But what it was, was a dictatorship.

CF: A Communist dictatorship, though. There are other kinds of dictatorship…

NC: Ceaușescu's personality cult was the most malignant thing.

CF: And wasn't that fanned by the Communists? What do you want to call them if not Communists?

NC: We can call them Alpinists: they wanted to climb up the ladder. I don't think we understand each other here. What Romania experienced was an absurd dictatorship that had nothing to do with the generous ideas of Communism.

CF: I would call them anything but generous. Paranoid, maybe. But I'll let it drop.

NC: As well you should.

CF: In postwar Romania, did you experience, did you feel anti-Semitism on your own skin?

NC: I felt it mostly during the War, when I was excluded from Romanian schools. Paradoxically, that concentrated us in a ghetto school, a school for Jewish girls, with Jewish teachers—absolutely brilliant teachers and students! One of us ended up teaching math at the Sorbonne, others became doctors, writers. I dare say they did us a favor.

I am now reading the memoirs of Emil Dorian, whose daughter Margareta was my friend in Romania, and with whom I reconnected here after many years—she left the country in '48, first for France, then for the US, where she published three books and appeared in *The New Yorker*. She also published a volume in Romania, *Herbarium*. Tall, thin, a plant herself, she taught botany at the University of Rhode Island. Her father, a minor poet of incontestable purity of soul and lyricism, was absolutely obsessed with the Jewish issue in his memoirs. I never had this problem—but then, I'm from a different generation. Some of the characters in my memoirs are people I know very well, like Tautu. I remember that once at a party I sang some folk songs—as you know, I have a whole repertoire at the ready. And Tautu said to me: "You are more Romanian than any of us." I was flattered by that.

CF: Who was Tautu?

NC: A minor poet we used to laugh about. We used to go to readings together, and he'd start with "Oh, green lady, green lady!"—supposedly an anti-Nazi poem, even though he had been a Fascist not too long before. I didn't know it at the time, yet his remark about my being so Romanian should have given me pause. But he was also an excellent practical joker. Some of his farces had genius in them: reactions were designed to reveal character. For instance, we were once on a boat. He and another writer had been in the army as part of a division which also included Soviets, and together they faked a broadcast of the National Radio on the ship: the Writers Union awards, live, supposedly. One poet, who was announced as having received second prize, threw a fit that she had not received the first prize and entered a fight with one of her closest childhood friends, another woman writer. A prose writer whose name did not appear among the awardees came out on the deck yelling: "Look at the sea! The sea, at least, is honest!" I wasn't listed for any award—I didn't like it, but I did not make a case out of it. The reactions to these practical jokes were phenomenal....

CF: This reminds me of Mircea Danieliuc's film *The Cruise*, which was not about writers exactly, but had all those award-winners for a stupid craft contest as part of the socialist propaganda.

NC: Precisely! His realist cinema was indeed extraordinary.

Heritage. Friends. Emotions

CF: You wrote your first poem and composed your first waltz at the age of five. Are you a confirmation that talent is inherited? Do you have artists in your family?

NC: There are, of course, instances of genius parents with mediocre children, mediocre parents of genius children, just as there are geniuses who come from geniuses and mediocrities who come from mediocrity. Far be it for me to despise mediocre individuals who have the same right to live as exceptional ones—unless they are envious, maleficent, or uppity (I have run into one of those, recently). I also have close to me a father and daughter who are both extremely gifted, but also a super-talented mother with ordinary progenies. Things happen.

CF: What was your relation to your father and your mother?

NC: My parents? They both had very little formal education—three or four years of high school. But they were doubtlessly talented. I adored my father. My mother used to sing Schubert, Schumann, or Brahms lieder in a little, precise soprano, accompanied by my father's rather un-exercised fingers on the piano. He used to write poems, too. My mother also, but comparatively rarely. He filled entire notebooks. His preferences ran more to entertainment poets, at least until he discovered Arghezi. My father taught me the splendors of the Romanian language, the taste for poetry and music. I once noted in my memoirs that it's a unique blessing to grow up cradled by the rhythms of poetry and great music. My father also passed on to me a trait that eased my way in life: humor. He was credited as an important translator—particularly from German. Yet the "apprentice" surpassed the "master" in both poetry and music. I am forever grateful to my parents, who fed and encouraged my evolution, even if after a certain point they stopped understanding my utterances or tonalities!

CF: What is the strongest emotion you remember?

NC: The strongest emotion I can remember now (there may well have been others, in such a long life) goes back to 1946. I was still living in my parents' house, and I had just taken an afternoon nap with my first husband, Vladimir Colin. My mother knocked on the door, saying that someone was on the phone for me. "Who?" I asked. "Ion Barbu," she said. I could not believe my ears. How could that be? My poetry idol calling *me*? The one who in my mind's eyes was the sovereign pontiff, the supreme magician who could conjure words simultaneously encrypted and explosive? He was inviting me to the famous Capsa Cafe to discuss my manuscript for *On a Scale of 1/1*, my debut collection of poems, which I had left with another writer for feedback. I can still feel that flashing emotion, a mixture of religious devotion, hope and terror, I feel it to this day running through my flesh—apparently, there are parts of my being that refuse to age.

CF: How was it at Capsa? What did you talk about? What did you eat?

NC: Though in my youth I used to be somewhat successful at drawing portraits, I do not dare compete with the portrait [the critic] George Calinescu made of Ion Barbu as a poet and mathematician in *The History of Romanian Literature*. When I met Barbu, he was 52. I was 22, and, in my youthful folly, considered him old. To be fair, my error was encouraged by his physical aspect: his thinning, greying strands of hair, a walrus-like mustache that covered his mouth to such an extent that I don't believe I ever saw his teeth, the uncertain shape of his body always hidden under a mound of clothes, his imperative walking cane which he hit against the floor for emphasis—and, then, his devilish eyes!

It's possible that he loved me, but I experienced all our meetings in a trance. I was green, overwhelmed by his attention—an attention of which I soon proved to be unworthy. I had an obscure desire to hurt him, a bout of sadism where he was concerned. One of his letters reminded me that I had a propensity to "torture inoffensive animals"—but, no, he was far from being inoffensive, his mentorship overpowered me, the mouse in me could not stand up to the elephant, it could only squeak deafeningly or nibble on his ear....

He dedicated two poems to me, which, together with his letters and the annotated manuscript I mentioned, are in the Library of the Academy in Bucharest. I dedicated only one to him, much too late, after his death:

To Ion Barbu

The One, the Great One,
loved me—I did not know, I was yet to grow
I stared at his bare pate (He was bald,
the Great One was auld)
his brows, intermixed,
his four-colored eyes
in their orbits fixed
and I did not know, I was yet to grow.

Had I known, was I grown
I should have licked
the ellipses of his feet,
scorched his mustache with my kiss,
like Mademoiselle Raging
I should have sought salvation through contagion.

CF: What about Marin Preda [one of the most prominent novelists of post-War Romania]?

NC: I've spoken a lot about Marin Preda. He played an incalculable role in my life. I did not love him enough to leave my husband at the time, Ali, whom I loved until he died. Marin never forgave me that.

I heard that some said he was ugly. In 1949, when I met him, he wasn't. He had an oblong, almost noble face, soft wavy hair, an intense gaze behind his glasses, carnal laughter. Anyway, I was never interested in beautiful men. He was worried about his hair—in 1953 he would wash it very often. He was modestly dressed, clean to the extreme, thin but not too tall. With age, his hair did indeed thin out, he put on weight, allowed himself to be dressed to standards imposed by his second wife, became ugly—but only on the outside. But in the years we saw each other often, I was not interested in his style.

I remember I translated Kafka's *The Metamorphosis* for him. Marin did not know French. Later, when he became famous as a writer, he abandoned the plain sorrel soups he had been doled out his whole childhood, and began ordering only filet of fish *"bonne femme."* I passed music on to him, too, especially Bach's St. *Matthew's Passion*, followed by the biblical text, in Romanian. Music stayed with him as a passion for a long time, he would listen to records to the irritation of his first wife, who, as she used to say, goaded him towards more "profitable" undertakings. He familiarized me with the great Russian prose of the nineteenth century.

What did all these women, his three wives, the women before them, me, find in him? He had a fascinating personality and was a profound thinker, he was able to sketch characters of friends and non-friends precisely and incisively and to evoke his childhood and adolescence with charm, he was an authentic writer who could reveal himself both naturally yet shyly and he had a great capacity for loving and suffering in love. Among his admirers was Paul Celan, another dear friend of mine.

Lastly (who's counting, and who says what comes last?), this was my personal experience with him, when, during a snowstorm in the winter of 1953, we were locked into a room at the Writers' Residence in Sinaia—I fictionalized it in my book *Fictitious Confessions*: "Dreary days of rain walled us into the house and into love, where I met him, and met myself through him. I would call those days complete: I fed on his absolute, astonishing nakedness. He had no cover, he had no protective immunity. I lived through the sacred moment of seeing this man as he had not been seen since his birth, in his disarming, total openness. One night, after the rains had passed, the moon invaded our bed and began caressing me. He followed the shape of my body, hovering the palm of his hand closely over my body, contouring it through the air, like a bird, like a satellite on a mysterious orbit, gliding, touching me with nothing else but the aura of his hand…"

CF: Maybe this could stand alongside the emotions you mentioned in relation to meeting Ion Barbu.

NC: Yes, maybe.

CF: You also counted Iordan Chimet [Romanian Surrealist writer] among your friends.

NC: Oh yes! But my friendship with him was not sustained by time. It was difficult to have a constant friendship with him. Sometimes he could not sustain it, at other times he would avoid it. He died of lung cancer, not of old age, but not before saving himself from the devastating March 4, 1977 earthquake in Bucharest.

I will tell you only one story, as Iordan himself told it to me: Veronica Porumbacu [Romanian woman poet known mostly for her Socialist Realist writings in the 1950s] was hosting one of her usual soirees on March 4, 1977. Ion Caraion did not go with his wife; he had a cold, so they escaped. B. Elvin [a Romanian Jewish writer of the early post-War period] didn't go either. Iordan decided to go, unannounced, to return some books he had borrowed from Veronica Porumbacu's husband. The husband received him in the doorway and did not invite him in. Perhaps he was afraid that Iordan would not mix well with the other guests. Offended, Iordan left the book and walked away. The earth shook half an hour later, taking down the building where Veronica Porumbacu and all her guests were.

CF: Destiny?

NC: So it seems.

CF: Do you believe in destiny?

NC: What do I know?

CF: I remember Iordan Chimet's book *An Anthology of Innocence*, which was published during a period when innocence was strangled, gasping for air.

NC: Even if intermittent—sometimes, years would go by—my relationship with Iordan Chimet was based primarily on moral and literary affinities. Then there was also our common friendship with Gheoghe Ursu [Romanian construction engineer, poet, and dissident] who was later beaten to death in jail. I cherished both very much. Iordan was a man of supreme daintiness: little mice, great fantasy, authentic innocence. He truly lived in his own imaginary homeland. I don't believe he belonged to our concrete, brutal world. He was always lost in fairy tales—I would have liked to do that too, to while my life away watching cartoons with little animals (not the super-technical ones).

CF: Tell me more about friendships. I believe they influence our state of mind, wherever we are.

NC: I had colossal friends. And losses equally colossal. For instance, Doinas [Stefan Augustin Doinas, a renowned Romanian poet known primarily for his work in the 1960s and 1970s], whose real name was Popa (he himself thought his pen name to be a little maudlin). I met him through his future wife at the time, Irinel Liciu, an exceptional ballerina and a spirit filled with intelligence, charm, and humor. She used to preface her interventions thus: "Well, I for one, though mostly concerning myself with legs…."

Doinas had been imprisoned for "failing to report" to the secret police: in 1956, when he was working for a theater magazine, a friend told him that students were going to protest in solidarity with the Hungarian uprising. After a year in prison, he managed to return to publishing. Before that, while he was part of a writers' group in Sibiu, he played a practical joke by signing a ProletKult poem as "Ion Motoarca"—and he received an award for that poem! He then published a quasi-conformist volume of poetry, after which, in the relatively relaxed atmosphere that followed the '50s, he became himself again. His cultural, intellectual stature was great.

Though he also experienced moments of disorientation in his prodigious career, his poetic authority was uncontested. We were friends for decades, with his wife Irinel, who modulated his rigidity—in fact, his rigor—even by dressing him up once as a lowly "Madam Moraru." We got to "corrupt" him at our New Year's parties in 2 Mai. What an irreparable double loss it was to see them both go, so close to each other! Same with the loss of the greatly talented prose writer Maria Luiza Cristescu, who used to say she wanted to end up like me—and to this day I have no idea what she was referring to: my age, my career?

Turn off that monstrous machine that is recording us, because I do not want to be misunderstood. I'm not afraid of what I have to say, but I'm afraid of what others may understand by it. Any friendship between a man and a woman must pass through the bed, unless one of the parties is reluctant or has a problem with it—I don't want to go into details. And it seems natural that it should be that way, especially for interesting and intelligent people. After all, intellectual and sexual flirtation are one and the same. They both signal strong attraction. And what is the point of resisting attraction, especially towards someone or something that's good for you? For your writing, for your mind, or for your body. But that's doesn't mean I was easy. On the contrary: I took matters very seriously.

CF: I know you are writing a strange and original dictionary, *My Dead*, where you draw portraits of people who were close to you.

NC: Yes, if only I could finish it before I join those people who were close to me!

CF: Are you afraid of death?

NC: I'm not afraid of death. I'm afraid of disease, of suffering, of mutilation, and, above all, of losing my marbles. But death, I'm not afraid of. In fact, I was once in a coma for three days, and I liked it! But then, I also liked coming back to life.

CF: How would you represent death? How would you draw it?

NC: I have no representation for it. No scythe, no black cloak, no white shroud, neither male nor female. The drawings I made during my lifetime have been portraits, self-portraits, or imaginary creatures orbiting Klee. But death is a natural phenomenon, especially when you die of old age or, as we say, you "die a good death."

CF: Do you still flirt with the idea of suicide?

NC: I didn't flirt with it. I thought seriously about it after the death of my husband Ali.

CF: Do you remember when we first met? It wasn't in Romania, nor was it in the US...

NC: Yes, it was at the Jerusalem Cinematheque. We were both guests readers. When was that exactly?

CF: Around 1993. You told me that night that you would commit suicide when you turned 70. "Why?" I asked you, visibly affected. You answered me: "Because Romania doesn't want to hear from me anymore. No publishing house asked me to publish my poetry after Ceaușescu fell..." At that time I was working for the publishing house of the Romanian Cultural Foundation—which later became the Romanian Cultural Institute. I went back to Bucharest and pushed for your book *The Undoing of the World* to be published. That was the first book you published in Romania after your exile in New York. I argued my proposal breathlessly: "If we don't do it, Nina will commit suicide!" A few older writers who knew you smiled knowingly: "Nina always says she's gonna commit suicide. Don't worry, she won't do it."

NC: Yeah, others always know what we are going to do better than we do, don't they? But I had brought some barbiturates with me to New York, just in case.

CF: One of them is with me, with your signature on it.

NC: I offered it to you because I trust you. Not for a purpose.

CF: I see it as a little pill of literary history.

NC: Whatever. I think the pills are past their expiration date. Like me.

Womanhood. Love life.

CF: Tell me about the distribution of power in a couple, from your perspective. Someone characterized you, simply, thus: "Nina loves poetry, strong men and Communism." How much of that is true, and how much of it is myth-making?

NC: For those who don't know me but think they do, or for those who built an artificial reputation for me, my answer may be surprising: I always yearned for a master, a tender and enlightened master, an authority able to lead me, to protect me, to get me through the practicalities of life (that's a blank chapter as far as I am concerned…). Of course, I had my own ways of being superior. The men I loved had their own, which always proved to be both complementary and harmonious to mine. Then, if course, there were bouts of "tyranny" on either side, from time to time, but without any kind of dramatic consequences. I never wanted to dominate, I always wanted to submit, though never slavishly—to subordinate myself with full respect of the laws of dignity.

CF: Do you think that you got as much as you deserved in love?

NC: At the time, yes. Now, I will answer you with an older poem of mine:

Questions and Answers

There was a time when I asked myself:
do I deserve to swim—light in lightness?
Now I no longer ask.
Nuder than my body
is my hive
with its rhombuses black and deserted.

There was a time when I asked myself:
am I entitled to so much love?

Now, I no longer ask.
The chambers of my heart are shattered.
Only the wind fools around.

That's all I'm entitled to.
That's all I deserve.
(Brenda Walker & Nina Cassian)

CF: Some claim that they loved multiple times in their lives, but only really fell in love once. What about you?

NC: Each time. I could not love without being in love.

Now turn that thing off so I can tell you something. I loved a beautiful man from Craiova. I'm telling you because that is your birthplace, and I, too, became tied to it, through my loved one. He was an engineer, but not the dry kind. Tall, blue eyes, he wrote poems, bad ones, but had the broad shoulders of a sailor. We loved each other devilishly. I could have stayed there for the rest of my life.

CF: Did he play a big role in your life?

NC: Oh no! Someone said I used to eat men for breakfast. Not a stitch of truth in that. It was men that ate my patience until nothing was left. I bored easily. I still have this quality. Or is it a defect?

CF: Were you a romantic?

NC: If I'm not mistaken, Marx was once asked what the main quality of men should be, and he answered: force. What about women? He answered: weakness. I too confess that my "romantic" views align me with an old, stubborn prejudice: I am (I used to be?) irremediably feminine.

CF: I can certainly confirm that. Someone once said that you are a woman's woman. I can see you flicking your hair, making long, graceful gestures, seducing through well-chosen words and, yes, through femininity, even now.

NC: Thank you. Though I can no longer recognize my body. Turn off that thing again. Honestly, I'm embarrassed to show my naked body to my own husband.

CF: What do you make of American feminism?

NC: I'm not up to date with feminism. But, despite my self-professed femininity within a couple, I identify completely with women's emancipation. Ever since my teenage years, it has infuriated me to hear men asking: "How many women composers are there? How many female philosophers?"—as if this handicap in numbers does not have explanations in history and is a mere consequence of a fundamental incapacity in the "weaker" sex to access such high disciplines of thought and creation! They do not ask about women writers, as they are overwhelmed by the evidence in that area. They do not know, or they pretend not to know that for centuries women have been either "objects of pleasure or beasts of burden" or, as the German saying goes, they need to limit themselves to the three K's: "Kinder, Küche, Kirche" (kids, kitchen, church), while males dominated these three areas, as well: *pater familias, chef de cuisine,* priest. The only "artistic" endeavors permitted to women, even in civilized societies and, obviously, only in privileged families, were learning a musical instrument and embroidery. Let us not forget that, in Europe, the last country to grant voting rights to women was Switzerland! Feminists claim equality between men and women—not equivalence! Women are physically weaker, have difficulties every month or after birth, which require extra attention and protection. Unfortunately, in a tremendous number of populations with fanatic religious groups, women are still humiliated, terrorized, tortured, stoned, and killed. What chances do our vehement protestations stand, even in the long run? Hard to say.

CF: On the other hand, I believe that feminism, while necessary and beneficial in the beginning, has killed femininity at least to some degree, in the great Western metropolitan areas. As if there wasn't enough competition in modern society, there is now competition between the sexes, and within the couple. The social, professional leap that career women have made is simply admirable, but there is a sense of urgency, of rush, associated with accomplishment, and successful singles can be more intimidating than seductive. Femininity, that mixture of force, fragility, and grace, is easier to find in old black and white photographs than in the glossy pages of business or fashion magazines. But sensitivity is not the same as weakness. Nor is success the same as happiness.

NC: True. I always liked wearing dresses, not pants.

CF: How did Maurice come into your life?

NC: If I were a believer, I'd say that his appearance in my life was a miracle. We met at a party organized by a common friend, poet Daniela Gioseffi. We talked, we got along, and we also liked each other. He was impetuous and compelling. He has stayed that way to this day. A few days later he sent me a card with two Dachshunds rubbing noses. How could he know that Dachshunds were my favorite dogs?! I had never mentioned that. It seemed extraordinary. And that's how it all started.

He came into my life late, when I no longer expected anything. I was impoverished, ugly, and old. He is a merry chipmunk, as you well know. Even I begin to think that I am lucky.

CF: How is life with Maurice?

NC: Full. Lively. We fight, too. He pushes me to write, to translate, to compose music. He cannot stand still. I learned a lot from him, we communicate the way I like to communicate. Now if only he were also Romanian....

CF: Did you ever want to have children?

NC: I don't remember. Maybe I did, but it wasn't meant to be.

CF: Yet you wrote a lot of books for children. Were you compensating? Or evading?

NC: I wrote them for myself. And for my friends. We are all children.

Humiliation. Betrayal.

CF: What was the greatest humiliation for you?

NC: I cannot remember.

CF: Constraints can humilate, as can betrayal, injustice, and lack of freedom.

NC: I cannot complain here, really. You bring up big ideas. Humiliation and shame come from small things, too. I was 14, and my friend Tamara asked me to lend her my *lie de vin* shoes to go to a party. I didn't let her have them. This pettiness followed me through life, I am ashamed of it to this day. Otherwise, since I have no money, I dress myself up from thrift shops or flea markets, and I am never ashamed. An old friend told me recently that she'd be humiliated to do that. Some people feel humiliation for nothing.

CF: Could your not remembering any humiliation mean that you suffer from vanity?

NC: I used to. I never became wise. Perhaps that's a waste of energy, but at least now I don't have that vanity anymore.

CF: Some say you're a narcissist.

NC: There was a time when narcissism could have come easy to me—I could have become a decadent absinthe-drinking poet. But I was saved by my Communist ideals, which were more humanist and more generous, and protected me from the dangers of idolatry and narcissism. I think I mentioned that before.

CF: I still don't think that Communist ideas can save anything.

NC: Well, I have to admit in all humility that they made me more generous, more accommodating. If they want to crucify me for that, they're welcome to do so.

CF: How did you weather break-ups? Did you ever feel betrayed or guilty?

NC: Each time I was jilted—and I was, on occasion, sometimes by a man, or a friend, or some circumstance—I always asked myself what I did wrong. And sometimes I would find an answer and judge myself guilty, while at other times I could not. More often than not, I tended to find myself innocent.

CF: What is the difference between walking out on a relationship and breaking up?

NC: When someone walks out on you, it's such a shock; there is nothing to prepare you for that. Break-ups have preambles, reservoirs of arguments and mental preparation which ensure that you are not surprised in the least bit. Leaving falls down, as they say, "out of the clear blue sky."

CF: But walking out on a relationship is experienced differently by the person who does the leaving than by the person who is left. There's a difference in energies.

NC: True. But that doesn't mean that both parties don't have something to lose. Walking out costs both parties, and is very painful. Especially when it's inexplicable. We are in one of those less fortunate professions in which we seek to understand things. But there are things that cannot be understood.

CF: Or explained.

NC: They just happen.

CF: All right, the two parties, the left and the leaving, both stand to lose, but is one of them placed on higher level of suffering?

NC: The one who is left suffers the most.

CF: The one who gets on the train and leaves feels more liberated once the train exits the station.

NC: Of course, and the one left standing on the platform is emptied out of a part of oneself, of events, of life.

CF: Perhaps it's also because the one who leaves is going towards something new, for better or worse, it does not matter. But any rupture brings about change. While the one left standing on the platform still inhabits the universe that used to occupied by the one who left. How was it for you?

NC: The truth is that I was left so many times, but I was never emptied out of life. I still had my memories. No one can empty me out of what I lived, felt, and refuse to forget. However great the pain or the stupefaction may be, they do not take away my dowry; I could try to erase everything and have a fresh start, but I do not want to. I could curate my memory, but that doesn't interest me. My memory is my most prized possession.

CF: Speaking of memory and memories, of things we think we are preserving and keeping intact in a coffer, don't you think that time plays a practical joke on us, that time molds itself to our shape and sometimes mystifies facts in a manner that's undetectable by us even as we are certain that we preserved a moment intact, the way it actually happened.

NC: How do you see that mystification going? Do you think that what happened to us did not actually happen?

CF: There is that possibility too, in the absolute.

NC: You mean it can all be our own illusion?

CF: Yes, some of our memories may well be invented. Sometimes we remember events we have not lived ourselves. Perhaps sometimes we want too much to have lived through certain things we have not experienced, and we come to remember them as if we lived them.

NC: Perhaps, in a more evolved spiritual level.

CF: You mentioned earlier that you are not interested in curating your memory. Sometimes memories adjust, round off reality, enhance our experiences in time.

NC: Yes, it is possible. Although I cannot deny, I cannot negate concrete events, words, exalted experiences. They did happen. Did I also have illusions? Yes, I used them to warm up, to sweeten the drama of separation or leaving or break-up—but not to such an extent that they erased and replaced what was real, live: gestures, words, miraculous encounters, moments of communication. I will not chase those away.

CF: I know, but time works as a two-way street: sometimes it erases, at other times it adds. I don't think anyone's memories are perfect transcripts of what happened—only, as you say, words, gestures, sensations, all "in search of lost time." Nor do I think diaries are open-door confessionals. Prudence, decency, considerations of what should be made public and what should not, all come into play.

NC: That may well be. I don't have the kind of ego that makes me believe I am completely objective. I may put a halo here, some embroidery there, or some knitting around the facts, but never to the point of forgery.

CF: Break-ups, departures, whether they have to do with people or places or situations—like, for instance, emigration—rupture something in us. Something dies or transforms inside us, maybe gets reborn, whether consciously or not. And perhaps we should try to evolve spiritually, to understand something from these separations, as from any suffering.

NC: What's left behind is the yeast, the suds.

CF: Memory is time, and, just like time, it's relative. It doesn't necessarily preserve the moments of exhalation or suffering in and of themselves. Rather, it keeps sensations, effects, and affects. It acts randomly, it amplifies and diminishes, or it simply takes a side road at times.

NC: What is there left for us to rely on then?

CF: Why do we need to rely on anything? Poets live with their heads in the clouds, or so they say. That makes them more vulnerable, perhaps. Also more buoyant. I also think that makes artists experience separations more intensely. Our states of mind are exacerbated by histrionics.

NC: I remember one of the accusations brought against me in a public trial which revolved around the Socialist Realist notion of the "typical." This was 1954, at the National Library in Bucharest. I said that trees ravaged by a storm are represented in poetry as more than just that—they stand for all trees, and the storm becomes layered with meaning, much more powerful than the actual storm described. My position was defending the conjuring powers of art, the fact that artistic expression synthesizes the experience of thousands or millions of people.

CF: And exposes us, too.

NC: Consequently, my position was considered an act of egolatry, of egocentrism, of positioning artists above all other things and people.

CF: Elitism was insufferable.

NC: Well, it still is, to this day. Here too, in the US. But then it's true: we accumulate experiences, feelings—all, forgive my big word, on a universal level. Shakespeare comes to mind. He too wrote, as they say in the movies, "based on actual events." Like that Romanian film, *The Death of Mr. Lazarescu*. That, too, is based on real events, but extends into the universal. If we have a gift, this is it: expressing a fundamental, universal truth that includes multiple experiences.

ROMANIA. AMERICA

CF: You mentioned *The Death of Mr. Lazarescu*. That is the film that opened up an appetite for the new wave of Romanian cinema, not only in the press, but also among a surprisingly large part of the American public.

NC: Surprisingly, yes, because that film has neither action, nor sex, not even physical violence, despite the rough realities it exposes.

CF: Another prejudice bites the dust: the one that holds that Americans only want Hollywood-type productions that satisfy their need for a happy ending.

NC: Precisely. We should be more trusting.

CF: And we should also drop the various clichés and what we think we know about this country.

NC: I, for one, have doubts. I still try to sniff out this place.

CF: Tell me what you sniff.

NC: I sniff some contradictions, a mixture of the intoxicating air of freedom and an obtuse need for limits. What I'm saying is a paradox, and I should not make any pronouncements because the decades I spent here do not mean much, especially in terms of my capacity to interpret things. I am not good at that, especially when it comes to politics. But my long nose—not an empty form, but a functional vessel—sniffs something unhealthy that started with the Bush administration. The air America breathed began to spoil just about then.

On the other hand, it seems that the American people, for the most part, are rather inert, in strange need of authority, and resistant to change.

CF: Still, after all, they made a spectacular change when they elected a

Black president. I believe Americans are generally disciplined, well-behaved, and trusting of authority because they have yet to live the kind of traumatic experience that compromises or undermines faith in authority and public institutions. They went almost directly from the Wild West to the era of technology and industrialization, and became trusting of those who led them here. They let their guard down.

NC: That may be, my dear Carmen, but I still think that they are rather inert. Complacent.

CF: A people concerned with daily noise, with relentless work…

NC: …and with that all-encompassing saying that says that all that matters is "making money and having fun." But here's the rub, as an old comrade used to put it back in Romania: what does having fun mean? Music, dance, food. But not necessarily a book, or classical music…

CF: A Broadway show, perhaps, where they can gobble up jokes impatiently.

NC: In cinemas, I hear people laughing when there is nothing to laugh at. Entertainment at any cost.

CF: *The Death of Mr. Lazarescu* was marketed as "the most acclaimed comedy of the year."

NC: An aside: when I moved here on Roosevelt Island 25 years ago, I stayed in an apartment across the street, on the other side of the tracks, with the old folks' home and the special needs housing. A very nosy neighbor rang my doorbell, came in, and looked everywhere—in the kitchen, the bedroom; she wanted to know everything she could about me. She told me to come down to the common room the next day at 12: you could win some cheese or butter or whatever in the building bingo game. Bingo! "Big fun!" she said. It must have been entertaining for her. Of course I didn't go, didn't get my cheese, didn't get anything. But that's a real obsession:

making some money and entertaining oneself, finding some reason to laugh.

CF: It is no less true that this society is consciously built on a positive, optimistic attitude. They're even positive towards negative things.

NC: They're rather infantile, which can also be pleasant evidence of innocence and purity. Like in Chimet's books.

CF: But children have their own way of figuring things out, their own antennas: a child recoils when something hurts him. One can tell if he doesn't like something.

NC: I know from tourists who visit our country—I mean our adoptive country, because that's my country now, despite the fact that I constantly miss Romanian food!—that Americans are perceived as friendly, or at least amiable. They always have a smile plastered on their face and are ready to talk about anything, even about things they know nothing about.

CF: On the other hand, elites are the same everywhere. And America has managed to concentrate not only on its own professional class, but also excellence from the world over. Yet I believe that it draws its strength not so much from exceptionalism, but, paradoxically, from that which draws the most criticism: standardization, uniformity. All the gas station convenience stores and delis, the fast food places and the houses and motels where you always expect the same degree of comfort, from New Jersey to Alabama.

NC: Well, yes, but New York is unique! You described it so well, it's no wonder you fell in love with it. Fatal attraction. What do you like best about it?

CF: In the beginning, everything and anything, all at the same time. I felt this was my place from the first day I got here.

NC: I discovered it gradually. You were lucky to have a choice. I never emigrated for economic reasons, or because of political discomfort. I was forced to seek asylum, against my will. Had it not been for Ceaușescu's dictatorship, I would not have stayed here. Even so, I never felt like I was really exiled, not even for one day. It soon turned out to be quite a sweet exile.

CF: What do you miss, or what did you miss at first?

NC: Nothing, now. But in the early days I missed the food, the friends, the language, the water, everything. That doesn't mean that I did not enjoy being in New York, which is an extraordinary city, and has very little to do with the rest of America, with all the small towns with their guns and their churches or whatever.

CF: What do you think is the biggest difference between Romania and America?

NC: The language. I went to see *The Death of Mr. Lazarescu* with a few American friends, and they all said that the film reflects not only Romanian realities, but also American ones. With one exception: the rudeness of doctors. That's something unheard of here.

CF: This doesn't mean that if you end up in a situation like his, with a past like his, in an emergency room at three in the morning, in a hospital filled with injuries from a pile-up, the doctors don't talk just like Romanian doctors, among themselves, in the room next door, outside of the patient's earshot. They just do it secretly, behind closed doors. There is great fear of malpractice suits, prudence is great, every statement can cost you. And then there is political correctness, which molds the minds of many people here.

NC : True. There is a kind of mélange here of perversity and puritanism.

CF: Words no longer are what they used to be for us: weapons, tools, vessels for communication. They are often protective screens. Where we come from, people are suspicious, not trusting that even the sun can give off light. That's how much the system changed us all. We managed to create a protective system that resisted any word that came from above. Authority had no credit with us. Here in America, on the other hand, authority carries a blank check. And I think that Romanian society, as profoundly perverted during Communism as it was, was paradoxically healthier in terms of freedom of thought for all of us grumbling, mumbling, grinning, ironic individuals. Our ability to ridicule, which is one of our most fundamental sins, actually saved us by serving as an escape valve.

NC: We took refuge in humor, parties, and alcohol…

CF: …And in the cafés. Yes, those were our own forms of resistance, of dissent. If we couldn't throw stones at the Central Committee of the Party…

NC: It's scandalous that we did not do that. I kept wondering why those who got close to Ceaușescu one way or another didn't inject him with something, didn't finish him off in some way…

CF: Well, surprise, they couldn't, or they couldn't even conceive of trying. There was a certain point at which official censorship turned into self-censorship. There was almost no need for surveillance; we spied on ourselves.

NC: I remember I had a cleaning lady right after I became a widow. I'd grumble constantly about the sinister couple who led the country, and she's day: "M'am, I don't want to talk about such things. I want to die in my own bed."

CF: Fear penetrated us to the bone, so much so that in the end the secret police did not have to do a whole lot of work. We were all turned in by colleagues, neighbors, office mates….

NC: In retrospect, I was pretty carefree: I spoke my mind to whomever happened to listen to me, though, in the end, it wasn't of much use.

CF: Do you think free expression is under threat and surveillance here, too?

NC: It's not going to change how I act. Freedom of expression? Democracy? They're all goners in America, too. Duplicity, philistinism, surveillance of calls and e-mails, and besides, I heard that using certain words in airports can get you arrested on the spot. Or deported. "Homeland Security" sounds a lot like Ceaușescu's Securitate, doesn't it?

CF: Were Romanian intellectuals of your generation arrogant or frivolous?

NC: Some were both. We played a lot. We'd do fortune cookies for New Year's with Gellu Naum [leading Romanian surrealist poet] and Petre Solomon [Romanian translator and literary critic]. Insults with no particular address: "When you talk you sound like a pigeon hawk" or "Your nerve is the kind I can hardly observe." That last one applies to me now—if ugliness was a virtue for me, old age is simply a disappointment.

CF: Do I dare ask you what you see when you look behind you?

NC: Dare ask. What I see is 88 delicious years.

CF: Are you content?

NC: Yes. I can honestly say that I lived my life well. I put on my own show, I did it my way, as they say, and I also did my duty. I had fun but I was also hard at work. Perhaps I could have written more if I was less lazy, if I sought enjoyment a little less, if I applied myself more. But then I loved and was loved. Love took up a lot of my time, but gave a lot of satisfaction back to me. I cannot complain. I had everything: recognition, insults, controversy, glory, exceptional husbands, all of them, plus the joy of writing, which has always been with me.

CF: Can I ask you for some advice?

NC: We're both very similar and very different. Aside from this transference of feelings, I have nothing to transfer to you. You are a strong personality. You believe in God, in luck, in destiny—which leaves very little space for your personal intervention—and that is one of the things that sets us apart: your belief in a superior being. I doubt there is one. But we are not adversaries. Only complementary beings. Two elements.

One piece of advice? Treasure your childhood!

The Last Phone Call
(April 5, 2014)

CF: Good morning, Nina. How are you doing?

NC: Stewing.

CF: How are you feeling?

NC: Terrible, but I won't complain. I'm fed up with myself.

CF: Let me read you some good news then: "On March 21, on World Poetry Day, the Palazzo Grimani Museum in Venice paid homage to Nina Cassian on the occasion of the publication of her bilingual book of poetry, one of the most important put forth by the Adelphi Publishing House…"

NC: Enough, little girl. Who cares? Had I been able to go to Venice, then it would have been different.

CF: You want to continue our dialogue through poems?

NC: Yes, we can duel and play. I always like playing with you through poetry. Let me pick something I like. And then I will also draw your portrait one of these days, if my hand will cooperate.

CF: Small, delicate hands you have.

NC: You mean I had.

CF: Fragile birds.

NC: Fragility is beautiful, but it has nothing to do with decrepitude. Old age is ugly and listens to no one.

CF: I thought we should launch our book in November.

NC: Don't count on me! As they say, we'll die to see another day.

Dialogues translated by Romanian born writer, director, and activist **Mona Nicoară,** who is currently working on a documentary film that explores the relationship between art, power, surveillance, and memory through the life of Nina Cassian.

The Promised Field

(Written on Roosevelt Island, where the poets were neighbors)

Nina
   Pointless I tell them: I am not the one
   I am not that, I have feathers and scales
   but also freckles—minuscule flat planets—
   also horns—but no, I am not the Beast;
   rather, I am a tamed fallen animal

Carmen
   Like a crooked letter of the Word
   I am only the animal sacrificed
   on the promised field,
   by me in myself exiled.

Slain by Words

Carmen
   I had begun to rise.
   The ceiling was parting.
   I was stepping life on life
   a bird on a knife's edge
   climbing without seeing
   my foot soles moistened in death
   fragile
   like the last one left behind

Nina
   That will not be the first—alas!—
   but the last breath of water
   of the murdered whale.
   How are we to ever find out
   who points the harpoon?
   Irremediably, we are in the blind posture
   of those felled by words, by ideas
   dangerous tools

Carmen
   which we swallow, amazed
   that we leave no trail of water

Said and Unsaid

Nina   Unspared by the fatal affliction called eternity.
It is difficult for us to describe ourselves.
We require a master portraitist
but, until that day, let us reflect in the mirrors
of river, icicles, tears, and blood dew,

Carmen   in the mirror
where words mingle our selves
angel and beast
said and unsaid

Memory

Nina   Increasingly ragged, the carnation,
fleshless and gaunt, the rose;
flowers aside, see the
skinned and plucked birds and animals,
see your eyes, your hands
or don't see. Lose sight of seeing.
Hands attempting to mimic motion

Carmen   turn to stone statues
purposefully made to simulate
youth without age or humiliation
life without meaninglessness
time does not flow
it melts like a icy knot in your throat.

Nina   And thus, from time to time,
Amid deterioration and massacres,
you glimpse the minute, green-gold image
germinating in a bean
left in a glass of lukewarm water.
Take in the sight as best you can
or, if you are not up to the task,
lose sight of seeing.

Birthday poems

Cassian and Firan were both born in November, two days apart.

rock and dew
to Nina

you sit on a lotus leaf and a bed of nails
every morning
you wash your memory with angel water
you undo the world with a slender arm
and swallow lost vanity
dipped in wax tears

time raps at the window with a cloven hoof

men and words and flow in your blood
loss and abandonment
small points of pride in a ground mirror

the hourglass draws back its hot sand

from the earth's eye socket
rushes forth a bird of rock and dew—
forever radiant
sublimely desperate

New York, November 27, 2008

A Quatrain
(though she deserves an entire ode)
for Carmen, on her birthday

Even Fantasy's Pegasus neighing is
Subject to exactitude's commands,
Always awake, always in a dream,
Luminous gift glowing from your skin.

November, 29, 2008

Poems by Nina Cassian

Selected by Maurice Edwards

Publisher's Note

Maurice Edwards' selection of Nina Cassian's poems is intimate and wise. He was, and is, the especially gifted lover and husband of Nina Cassian. He made the last years of her life more Cassian-ly livable. As long as I've known him, some 65 years, Maurice has had a history of flying, alone or in flocks, around the spheres, choirs, and bedrooms where music and poetry embrace. His mortal history you can find in the Yellow Pages is: Maurice Edwards performed on Broadway; he played in *Threepenny Opera, Fiddler on the Roof,* and *The Golden Apple,* etc. He was co-founder and program coordinator of *The Cubiculo.* Edwards was managing director as well as artistic and executive director of the Brooklyn Philharmonic Orchestra (1971-1999). Since his retirement, he has served as artistic consultant to the New York Virtuoso Chamber orchestra.

Edwards and Cassian were married for more than fifteen years. Edwards published a memoir called *Revelatory Letters to Nina Cassian* (OCC Art Gallery Press 2011). Cassian's *Continuum* is dedicated "To Maurice Edwards, my husband, who almost forced this book out of me, helping my essential survival."

S. M.

The Inclined Plane

Up, up, with an as yet undefined movement
probably called translation—have you ever seen
the infinite procession of slaves carrying enormous blocks
which, for their part, will for all time
bear the majestic name of pyramids?
Down, down, have you ever felt the first breath
of the avalanche, the delicate slivers and dust,
barely moving, ingenuous, putting forth a gesture
of destruction
and beginning to shake the world's foundations?
A single plane, inclined, toward what?
Toward the x-axis,
toward the y-axis,
and all the other conventions,
toward something rising and something falling;
the slope alone—you can clamber up or slide down.

Do you remember gliding on a gray tongue of concrete
toward the green glottis of the sea?
Do you remember touching the surface of that sea,
and breaking it,
going down through it, feeling a perpetual slope,
                              an inclined plane?
It takes a long time to crawl back up and break the surface
because time, there in the depths, has no orifices,
                              no nostrils, no pores:
it is an obdurate time—a kind of eternity.

Slides, chutes, inclined planes, oh, tragedies—
for tragedies are not obligatory; they are tragic
precisely because they could have been avoided—
so neither the vertical nor the horizontal really exists—
only a great inclined plane.

Have you ever struggled to get up with your fingers
clenched in the mud that lies between you and the horizon above?

You looked at that pure, cold, cutting skyline
and quickly at the earth in front of your mouth,
then again at the horizon, and at the short blades of grass
that spring between the fingers clenched in that mud.
You fell and struggled again on that treacherous slope
without any other point of support but your own elbows,
kneecaps, heels, and your own forehead
soiled with earth mysteriously like an old manuscript.

The great plane rocks back and forth,
at one end a king, at the other a boar,
at one end a huge block of salt and at the other a book,
at one end a house, on the other a river,
and finally the great plane
rocks with old people and snowfalls,
padlocks, watches, blue leaves, melodic scepters,
horses and ships swinging, death's temples rocking, rocking,
quiet alcohols reeling, balancing.

I stand crucified on a plank, aware
                              of the continual flow of life.
And here I am, incapable of stepping twice
                              into the same stream.
I myself am beginning to pour forth like a spring,
                              my hands prolonging themselves,
my hair, the tail of my eye, flowing down,
then up onto an inclined plane,
my whole being in a procession of ovoid cells, pulsating,
existing, not existing, ending briskly, continuing smoothly—
have you ever seen a floating cross?

It is a bird flying obliquely
over the oblique axis of the globe.
I rest my head in my left palm,
slightly inclined, contemplating, contemplating
The Great Inclined Plane.

(Naomi Lazard)

Greed

I am greedy. Puritans scold me
for running breathlessly
over life's table of contents
and for wishing and longing for everything.

They scold me for feasting
on joy and despair, together
with jugs of sour cream
and hot polenta.

They object to my wearing a tie pin
and a carnation in my hair,
for being sometimes boy, sometimes girl,
and who knows what else!

They rebuke me for not distributing love
according to a plan, for not rationing it,
for having a potter's agile hands
and now and then solving equations.

Well, that's my way! I'm hungry, I'm thirsty,
I rush through the world like a living sound.
I refuse to walk slowly, to crawl,
or to remain indebted for a kiss.

I'm greedy, I gulp things down, I fly,
and I'm proud that on my small lapel
occasionally a decoration glitters—
call it rapture, that golden rosette.

(Stanley Kunitz)

Ballad of the Jack of Diamonds

Here is the Jack of Diamonds, clad
In the rusty coat he's always had,
His two dark brothers wish him dead,
As does the third, whose hue is red.

Here is the Jack of Diamonds, whom
The fates have marked for certain doom.
He is a mediocre fellow,
A scrawny jack whose chest is holly
And spattered with a dismal yellow-
No model for a Donatello.

The two dark brothers of this jack,
Abetted by a third, alack,
(Who, draped in hearts from head to foot,
is the most knavish of the lot),
Have vowed by all means to be free
Of him who gives them symmetry,
Making a balanced set of four
Whose equilibrium they abhor.

One brother, on his breast and sleeves,
Is decked with tragic, spade-like leaves.
The next has crosses for décor.
The motif of the third is gore.

The Jack of Diamonds is dead,
Leaving a vacuum in his stead.

This ballad seems at least twice-told.
Well, all Romanian plots are old.

(Richard Wilbur)

Lady of Miracles

Since you walked out on me
I'm getting lovelier by the hour.
I glow like a corpse in the dark.
No one sees how round and sharp
my eyes have grown
how my carcass looks like a glass urn,
how I hold up things in the rags of my hands,
the way I can stand though crippled by lust.
No, there's just your cruelty circling
my head like a bright rotting halo.

(Laura Schiff)

Tirade for the Next-to-Last Act

I'm leaving you, I won't touch you anymore.
I've run out of things I have to prove to you,
so there's no reason to postpone the drowning
of molecules called hands or eyes or mouth
in the patient earth which waits—but not for me.
Earth knows it owns me, right to horizon-zero.
I've told you almost everything I know;
even the lie I told was a pious lie
because it leapt to life, came into being
embodied as a leaf, or as a rabbit,
and I cannot reject a living creature.
Also, I leave you because I am so weary
of the way the century melts in the one before
as if the milk the child sucks from its mother
went back into her breast—or worse than that,
as if the brow of a philosopher
kept sloping back till it rejoined a species
long extinct, and hirsute, and prehensile.

I've picked up information on my way
but none of it from scholarly pursuits
or from the established canon of great books;
mostly from heat and cold, from birth and death,
all that comes past us only once, alas,
so it's no guide for what will happen next.
I remains as vulnerable as ever,
knowing a thousand objects by their names,
a thousand states of mind I cannot name.
I don't see their utter metamorphoses,
I didn't notice when they took their leave,
abandoning me to confusion,
as if dropping into a pool of blood.
So I'm leaving; I won't touch you anymore.
You've said so many times you can't abide me

though I drew my portrait for you with such care,
relying on the way you had sketched it out.
But I'm incapable of imitation,
or so it seems. I lack the talent
to resemble you—much less, myself.

My smiles are always misconstrued as grins.
And when I laugh, all heads are turned away
as if I had committed some indecency.
I pick the wrong occasions for my tears:
when the crowd cheers a city holiday.
When I sculpt a statue, everyone screams,
"He has made himself into a graven image!"
When I shrivel with a serious illness,
I'm not believed: it's the devious way
my sad body causes an obscure epidemic . . .
So I'm leaving you, goodbye. Goodbye, I leave.

(Carolyn Kizer)

Serenity

There'll be a time, serene, a time for hymns.
I'll underline the air with just one gesture,
and I will utter stainless words.

I will say "sky" and "brook" and I'll say "sun"
and "tear" and "music" and "immunity."
There'll be a time, a time when memory
of massacres won't reach me anymore,
turning instead into a distant breeze of poetry
as sometimes blood itself exhales.

From all that once had been promiscuous,
only the sacred will remain, and I will praise
the contrasts, reconciled, forgiven and forgiving.
So I'll say "sky" and "sun" and "music"
and sky will be, and sun will be, and music
will be around me and around the world.
I'll let the vowels all regain their halo.

And it will come, that bright, sonorous time,
a time solemn and pure, a time for hymns,
and it will come, that time. Indeed it will!

Kisses

Our kisses, hundreds, thousands—
even millions—who knows!
I never counted them:
my fruits, squirrels, carnations,
rivers—my knives!
I could sleep and dream on your mouth,
sing and die there,
again and again;
that mouth—deep harbor
for a night's lodging after a long journey,
reaching it, yet still longing to reach it . . .

There are battles—our kisses—
heavy, slow, hurtful,
where blood, voice and memory all take part.
Oh, how jealous I am of the water you drink
and of the words you speak—
of your blue sighs . . .
Jealous of those unjust
partings of our mouths!

(Brenda Walker and Andrea Deletant)

In an Old English Inne

I'm cold,
useless,
sometimes drunk,
wasting my working vacation
near a fireplace, its coals burned out,
and a black cat—
talking to myself
and sometimes to the cat.

This realm is possessed by sundry ghosts,
some bearded, some feathered,
some just naked
like long, transparent fingers
playing an invisible score.

Cold, useless, drunk
and talking to myself
—while the cat's only activity
is purring.

Night of Revelations

Where is my lovely smile now,
that foolish and divine smile of mine,
like an aroma from my features,
so much so that it might have generated
a sect of smilers whose deity I would become?

Indeed, it fascinated the weak-spirited
by an immobility so solar
that is seemed to be the movement
--both static and vertiginous—
of Fate itself.

Mine was the smile of the golden idol
for whom wrath, forgiveness, love, indifference
bore the same expression
like a universal scent of matter.

One night I realized
that I wasn't smiling anymore.
My face was void,
and a terrible absence weighed on it.

The world was pressing down on my face without letup.
My smile no longer opposed it.
I made weird gestures. Someone looking at me
would have thought I was wrestling the Invisible Man.

And as it weighed on my face, the world
dug into the middle of my forehead,
on just that spot where, it is said,
the Third Eye should appear.

And yes, at dawn, there it was—
the eye all by itself, shining alone,
the eye standing eye-to-eye with itself
—an eye for an eye, —
the eye in the bird's eye view,
from every point of view.

Fall in New England

The glass shrivels,
the birch tree senses its loneliness
and the spiders hide in the fold of my nightgown.

Yesterday, on the stone terrace
in front of the sculptor's study,
I froze in the Nordic breath;
a sound of cold, long as a horn,
linked one hill to another.

Then the dogs came.
Black, gentle.
One of them put his head on my lap.
His head was heavy as a horse's head.

Blue, boreal flames completed the picture.

Licentiousness

Letters fall from my words
as teeth might fall from my mouth.
Lisping? Stammering? Mumbling?
Or the last silence?
Please God take pity
on the roof of my mouth,
on my tongue,
on my glottis,
on the clitoris in my throat
vibrating, sensitive, pulsating,
exploding in the orgasm of Romanian.

(Brenda Walker and Andrea Deletant)

Tristia & Inferno

I refuse to climb and to descend
those paths
to make this place more familiar to me,
this place everybody talks about,
though nothing ever happens here.

I prefer to be exiled like Ovid
(whose nickname "Naso" fits my nose)
though not at a fiendish seashore, the Pontus Euxinus,
nor between hills almost bald,
with just one wart or a tuft of hair
from long-gone forests.

I prefer to be exiled like Dante
(with whom I share the profile),
but not from eternal Rome,
rather from my vanishing childhood
in which many things happened,
but are never mentioned.

Actually, here I am, exiled
between a pregnant yesterday
and an aborted tomorrow.

The Big Conjugation

I, who never had any appointed functions
except the function of reproduction, I never deserved of anyone
but you, fair Isolde, infinite daughter of my womb,
—I, who never had any worldly ambitions
except the ambition to turn the frosty letter "I"
into the ecstatic sword separating Isolde from Tristan,
—I, who never had any chances except the chance
to live smiling, when, instead of hair or memories,
insults and spit were running down my temples,
—I, who was never in power, but had the power
to exist and to embrace you, my enemy,
and to be ready at any time to die,
—I've always had the "Haves,"—having,
had, have had, had had and Have.

Promises

I wrote a promissory note
intended to pay off my debts.
However, all I had left
was my dead childhood
in its tiny coffin.

Though not a demagogue,
in my adolescence,
I promised humanity
a harmonious existence,
like a majestic chord and accord
—but I couldn't keep my word
because the rulers of this earth
are all tone deaf . . .
Now, finally, I promise myself
—since the remaining rags of my life
continue to deteriorate—
to die in style, peacefully,
with a smile . . .

2006

Tyrants

I knew only a few of them personally.
Between me and them
—like a protective deity—
stood my colossal ignorance,
a bodacious woman of stone,
related to the Statue of Liberty,
my dignity,
part of the Infinite Column.

It happened, nevertheless,
in a moment of recklessness,
I was touched by one or the other
of those tyrants.
Their glare dug
invisible craters into my flesh,
They shoved me about
with their padded shoulders.

They are responsible
for all the tombs
archeologist discover in me.

However remotely I stood from them,
my destiny seemed to be that of an obedient dog
listening with ears pricked up
to their commands.

Seemingly . . .

Utopia Unlimited

These tools were good, at first,
to cut, to slash, to stab—but then
they seemed too petty, too inefficient.

So other tools were soon invented,
which could wipe out a man
as easily as you wipe off a stain,
making him vanish—nobody would care—
in the transparent coffins of the air.

These tools were called weapons of mass destruction.
And if iron was not used to make a plow,
and if steel did not give birth to bridges,
it is because they were hungry for death.

But this was long ago and far away,
when there was always war on earth.
Indeed, it's hard for us to understand—
for us who live, for centuries, in peace . . .

But blood, a stubborn witness, takes the stand.

A New World

I had a lot of good friends,
insane like myself.
We attended gatherings,
but society intrigued against us
until we became enemies.
We bit ourselves, we poisoned each other,
we lost the idea of the immortal waltz
in time's ballroom.
The gray gent and the bald soprano
cursed away at each other.
Mr. Professor died,
asphyxiated by his own gas stove.

The intellectuals fight
head to head.
The proud one and the humble one
scutter unintelligibly.

Dear Hyperion,
What a phenomenon!

Summer X-Rays
(Romania in the 80s)

I

Fabulous days
with endless swims,
with algae around my waist
and convex tears on my cheeks.

Far away on the shore;
children shouting,
dogs with golden rings
circling their muzzles,
and rumors of abandoned memories.

I know what's awaiting me—
the winter of my discontent.
I have a reservation
outside on a hard bench
holding a bag of frost-bitten potatoes.

That's why I swim so far out,
willing prisoner
inside the sea's immense green magnifying glass.

II

Despite all my inner crumblings,
I'm still able to recognize a perfect day:
sea without shadow,
sky without wrinkles,
air hovering over me like a blessing.

How did this day escape
the aggressor's edicts?
I'm not entitled to it,
my well-being is not permitted.

Drunk, as with some hint of freedom,
we bump into each other,
and we laugh raucously
on an acutely superstitious scale
knowing that it's forbidden.

Could it be just a trap
this perfection
this impeccable air,
this water unpolluted by fear?

Let's savor it as long as we can:
quickly, quickly, quickly.
.

Epilogue

Between the sun and me
there is a veil of quietude
which protects my eyes
from the scratch of light
which spares my being
from the blister of knowledge
which allows my self
to breathe undisturbed.

So now the war is over
and now the love is over.
How beautiful the death
well prepared in advance.

Shedding

A curl, one curl plays at the nape of my neck
wiping my face like treasured furniture.
Only the curl is young in this waste
where drawers break apart—by nothing
but maybe by music!
Can this curl be starting a dance
that a shoulder, a hip, an eye could join
if detached and finally free?
Again I crumble into oblivion.
Now's the time to set my cells free.
To let them leave my being.

Bon voyage, eyes!
Bon voyage, eyelashes!
Bon voyage, dancers!

(Laura Schiff)

The Kiwi Bird

I am the Kiwi bird
the one without wings...
Don't speak to me,
Don't call me.
I don't understand you...
Because I can't fly
and because some children
throw stones at me
I've become dumb.
My beak opens sometimes by itself,
as if I were thirsty
as if I were sick,
but I'm neither sick nor thirsty.
I am only dumb,
very very dumb.
Other times, however,
I think I hear something,
something like the flapping of a sheet in the wind,
or a wing in flight,
and then I walk a little
I raise my stiff leg
and my step seems suddenly alert
but I immediately sit down on the ground
and with my long beak,
I begin to scrach my wingless back
scratch, scratching as if
there were nothing left in the world
but me and my beak that pokes.
I'm the Kiwi bird that can't understand.
Don't speak to me.
Don't call me.

Once very few years, it happens
when the moon seems to hum, and ring in a certain way
that shame and sorrow, my only emotions
start glimmering in my flesh,
and then I want to hide
and I have nowhere,
and I twist and bend
and I have nothing with which to cover myself.

I am the Kiwi bird
the one without wings.

I am the Kiwi bird.

(Laura Schiff)

Shock

You threw me on a field of metal
on a burning field of metal
that mirrored my fall
and I watched the falling
the wounds doubling
and I smashed against my own pain
as against a true enemy.

(Laura Schiff)

Ecstasy

On the moon's stripe the goldfish meet.
Look, a mad piling mass,
tails dissolving like soft snow.
In the cold gold wine of the sea, giddy.
A pale mute frenzy flows from their mouths.
Goldfish in gold wine, in magic moon,
noiselessly drunk,
glide past the drum of the ear, the air,
and etch with tails digits of light.
A dazzling swarm drowns.
Their bulging eyes repeat the moon
a thousand times scattered in waves, a thousand clusters of
grapes, grapes, grapes, grapes, grapes.

(Laura Schiff)

Pain

God, how they shrieked,
how they sobbed
the night birds.
God, how they cackled!
Wide eyed,
I stared into the dark,
and on every rooftop,
the sea birds
clacked their beaks.
What an orgy of laughter!
The cold jeers
searched for me
in the solitude.
God, how they cackled,
strange city dwellers,
the night birds.
This is pain,
I told myself, keeping vigil.
This is how it hurts.
Deafening
silver wings,
voices, beaks, claws,
long knives in the night,
beaks by the window...
...you were far
our love over.

(Laura Schiff)

The Cripples

When the cripples hurl their crutches in the air
the sticks beat our heads, our sound heads.
Yet only we rush to grab them
a second before they topple,
we who stand bruised
till they stop whimpering,
these cripples draped in our arms.
They stain us with urine,
they gouge us, they sigh
in our ear something obscene,
and we keep propping them up.
But if we had never meddled
we'd see them running, flying
jeering, hopping agilely on one leg,
snatching their tumbling crutches—
the crutches they'd die without—
for what else can they hit with?

(Laura Schiff)

Useless

No. You didn't need my gestures
like some ribbons wrapped around doorknobs
nor my glances embroidered on drapes
nor my whole playful universe.

And you didn't need the high harmony
of some lone word, nor perfect desire
with its pale chisel sculpting
the stone of moments to a kiss.

I was useless to you like reversing
three seasons or only two
like the fall of rain into glasses
like raindrops splashing over books.

(Laura Schiff)

Self-Portrait

I was given this strange triangle face,
this icicle head, this face
for the prow of a pirate's ship
with long moon-like hair on the skull.

I was given to walk this violent shape
wandering from night to day,
wounding the retinas of any who see
the incongruous shadow I make on walls.

What am I? Ancestors, kin reject me.
Briefly they join with races
black, white, yellow, red to reject me.
Even the species won't have me.

And only when I'm hurt and scream
and only when I freeze
and only when time fills me with sin
—they call me beautiful,   They call me human.

(Laura Schiff)

Poems by Carmen Firan

Selected by Nina Cassian

loneliness in two

I invited loneliness to dinner.
Seven on the dot. Top button on the intercom,
name faded, though untouched for some time.
Off the elevator, third door to the right.
Bell's broken.
Doormat's worn. By time. By nothing.
It drizzles. Intently.
Rivulets furrow the windows.
It's foggy and cold. Just like that fall morning
in the mountains, when you tied on your boots by the bedside
and claimed you simply had to climb those peaks
though no one was waiting
and nothing was there for you
but the ashen sky riven by my tears,
rivulets staining stones.

It's after seven. By now the candles stand shorter,
the wine has forsaken the glasses,
silence hisses like a bullet fleeing the gun.

Then loneliness arrives. I hear her shuffling. I jump to the door,
press my ear against its cold wood.
A mountain thrusts up in my chest.
The meat too has grown cold. The plates
have exhausted themselves.

Then, she pokes her head through the smokescreen.
She caresses my hair. Then moves on.

(Mihaela Moscaliuc)

the other side

how love passes
like summer
like a fox among unripe grapes
her hair turns amber
so she may slip unseen though the tall grass
light-footed
stealthy
to the other side

(Mihaela Moscaliuc)

spider

this one morning I grew, all by myself,
more than in all the years
I shared with you
my arms pushed out of the nightgown
long as bean stalks
silk threads drawn skyward
by a skinny spider
I snatched the moon and hid it under the bed
inside a box of photographs shot at the seaside
I raided paradise, searching for you, and hell too

the sky lay empty
or maybe the emptiness was mine

(Mihaela Moscaliuc)

blending

the native ocean and this foreign ocean
the one that washes your ankle and the one that buries it
the sand that sifts through the delicate neck of the hourglass
and the sandstorm that reddens your eyes
the tentative horizon and the strict borders
waves fulfilled at the shoreline
and the sun broken at dusk
by a scorched cliff

the native blue and this foreign blue
that tastes of gentian and algae
both seep into the blood
blending
so you may not remember them

(Mihaela Moscaliuc)

dialog

you're beautiful, you said, beautiful as autumn,
beautiful as a still life with dove and wooden table,
you're the birch itself, the speechless birch,
its growth stunted.

Part the waters of your shirt,
unspool the latticework
let autumn bleed, drop by drop,
onto your long neck.

(Mihaela Moscaliuc)

sleep is not my own

o, lord, Death fears me
he touches me lightly
then jumps away like a child
and trembles
his finger on my lips
not disingenuous as it might be
gentle and whole he smiles at me

I take his hand and force him
to stroke and caress my sleep
as it lies stretched on a bed sheet

his hand draws back:
I can't—he whispers—
your slumber is too cold
and yet, and yet
something in you draws me,
and I could hold you
and I could tell you tales and tales,
your eye draws me,
I am inside its globe,
teach it silence
I fear its looks
and I can't hear or see myself

(Andrei Codrescu)

tea for one

the most difficult thing to learn
is to live alone
to put under tree bark
the body of the newborn
from which a new tree would grow

to seduce your time
like a capricious lover
who will betray you
with another woman's age
with the Father's image
descending on the face of another man
but just as unyielding

the most difficult thing is to drink your tea
in the morning together with your solitude
and to gaze at her thin fingers
stirring the sugar in your cup

(Julian Semilian)

festina lente

it is always too late
even the philosophy of the Greeks
must be taken with a grain of salt
you can plunge sink without a trace
and your body weight
will not raise the level of the ocean,
the weight of your soul is valued at .0003
and this only if you die forewarned
by the eternal festina lente

things are always much simpler:
a baby's cry, the air of a summer night,
the books from which all that remains
is the happiness of a few synonyms,
the regret at the end
that love gives you everything
but time

(Julian Semilian)

what remains

poetry,
a rare snake,
binds hands and learns how to perform
coiling insidiously
in the service of power

but wait, don't throw
the mantle of clouds off my shoulder
remember, in the beginning was the word,
at the end, the word distorted

eventually
there will only remain
poetry, a blue snake,
insinuating itself
into our full cup of tears

(Isaiah Sheffer)

suppositions

what would the savior have looked like
grown old
would he still have lent
his severe, nostalgic face
to the builders of churches
to the arrogant destroyers in quest of myths
or guilty would he have healed
his own joints
letting the water remain water
while the blind fumbled along their way

would he have given his last son
to doubt
or in the evening
laying his head on Magdalene's knees
would he have seen the earth as round
spinning on her index finger

(Adam J. Sorkin with Carmen Firan)

flight tracks

in every dream I speak a different language
and in every language words have a different color
blind dreams rise from my forehead
inflated on the purple horizon

from all I said in my lives before and to come
there remain only the flight path, the wing's whisper
the island where I took refuge
free, o free inside so many walls
on which I scratch neither hearts or love-words
but signs in the language I speak while asleep
a dialect of Old Angelic still useful for crossing borders

I have a vocation for happiness
a sort of unconscious facility
at making an ally of the caretaker of dreams
who's always ready to lend me the silk cocoon
in which words sneak past customs
intimate objects I carry with me undeclared

nothing's to be done about my golden dowry
dead languages yield just the powdery dust of stars

(Adam J. Sorkin with Carmen Firan)

soon

I'll grow old.
soon.
you won't hear me.
snow will cover my traces.
one morning I'll wake up beside you
and open the curtain
convinced that through the window
I can see the Himalayas from above—
a cynical miracle achieved without the least effort.
lion cubs will spring forth ravenous
tear out my heart bolting it down.

you don't believe in the devouring word
you'll hear only the crunch of the poem
in their young jaws.

(Adam J. Sorkin with Carmen Firan)

eclipse

everything passes, you told me,
as when on a high-speed train you look out the window
and the trees rush behind you
with the mist of each word on a winter morning

everything passes, you said,
with the thick soup dribbling from grandma's chin
to the edge of a hospital bed
with a pressed violet in an encyclopedia
whose pages no one will ever turn

everything passes,
the waters grows calm
the blare of sounds will blur—
the shadow sets upon the body

(Adam J. Sorkin with Carmen Firan)

crack-ups

in my late thirties I killed my ego
in the bathroom
I slowly twisted its neck with my own two hands
the Adam's apple thudded to the cement floor
one by one I cut the threads
from which I drew my power
strong enough to keep me upright in a hunchback world

I knew I was mistaken to love my crack-ups
more than the patch of earth granted to me
now I know that each departure
is nothing more than the self-importance
of not being the one who stands
waiting on the platform
a tree grown in the cracks of the asphalt

in cold blood I watched the warm, proud, salty stream
snake down its chin
washing away the arrogance of forgiving nothing
the sweet venom of my daily solitude with an impudent body
the bread and butter of my youth

(Adam J. Sorkin with Carmen Firan)

letter from the world's metropolis

you'd think we're not so alone
among so many secondhand champions

an exiled poet left the faucet on
out of toxic words grow flowers
whose color has swallowed their perfume
gardens of plastic and cardboard
patriotic melancholy supersized
for prizes bought on a summer vacation

we're told to drink plenty of water
the empire is whitening its teeth rejuvenating
and labors tirelessly for those ambushed
by immortality and depression
well behaved, we are mute and blind
astonished not to find in our guide to manners
the Romanian word *dor* we much long for

at MOMA the DaDa exhibition flatters our history.
Friday evenings admission is free.
and so are we.

(Adam J. Sorkin and Carmen Firan)

on the other side

I'm writing to tell you:
keep away from death

she'll come again anyway
wrapping her egg
in a nest of bright wires
run as far as you can
every evening around nine
when her finger weighs down
the hand of the alarm clock
another dead weight
this old man a bit to the right,
that woman even farther,
a row of birds on the window ledge
pecking at my heart

she guards your threshold
like a trusty watchdog
lest you lavish too much of yourself on this world
that needs no more than
your name on a sheet of paper

I snap her spine
and flee as far as I can
she helps me cross the street
she knows me by sight

on the other side
a silent black dog sits and waits

(Adam J. Sorkin with Carmen Firan)

hemispheres

yes, only you can love me
just the way you do
staring directly into my brain,
scratching your fingernail
across one hemisphere,
a secret mimosa
arrogant and vain,
and telling me I'm beautiful
as I sit at death's table,
with a bouquet of neurons
preserved in a vase

never will I be so lonely
as when I'm with you
hormones float by,
stick to the walls,
objects wail in shame

but you love me the way you do
you clasp my head between your hands
and tell me
you've known me for eons
since many a sea
disappeared into the land

in secret I dream
of not crying on your shoulder
with my left brain

(Adam J. Sorkin with Carmen Firan)

to the very last

the loved ones
and those not loved
depart one by one

the sand slips through our fingers
to the very last grain

even the heart of the poet
freezes up

let thy will be done
and give us not
so much death
in one single life

(Julian Semilian)

almost the same

after a while I began to resemble you
I saw the same patterns
in the ceiling's cracks
the same huge prehistoric beasts
in the white clouds
of a summer sky in the country,
I flicked my cigar the way you did
fingering an imagined guilt

my left eye migrated to your left eye
my hand grew at the end of your arm
we stroked the dog one after the other
and he never knew
which was me, which were you

(Adam J. Sorkin with Carmen Firan)

differences

the difference between solemnity and a rigid pair of shoulders
is the same as between pretended silence and speechlessness
the parallel lines race each other leaving no trace on the skin
they flow between heaven and earth
linking big infinity with small infinity

the difference between loneliness and a languorous woman
recumbent on a divan
is the same as between imposed exile and running in circles
far enough from home

with your fate recast halfway through your journey
in the midst of others' silence
you could die and no one would hear

(Adam J. Sorkin with Carmen Firan)

it snowed

sometimes
He descends through my soul
in my chest I feel the earth's weight
under His heel
pressing on mine

in the lightened sky
a firm line
a sword will fall
under it my slender throat settles

one sudden morning
man was given the Word
that reigned alone

one sudden morning
you part the curtain
and see that it snowed
what more can you do,
what else can you do?!
it snowed—that's all

the curtain wraps itself
around your throat

(Andrei Codrescu)

the woman of sand

I would like to have been wise
to be spared having to discover
there are no sins
that our passage through life wasn't on purpose,
to believe in the destiny
of the melancholy conquerors
turning wine into blood or water
and to speak with reserve
frightened by all the old proverbs,
saws and warnings told by the wise
who never respected anything but genius
and preserved nothing except flawlessness
from which the cynics nurse their eternity
the way the ocean follows its sensuality
and always sips from the beach
some woman of sand
in the most beautiful life possible
I hold with my breast the noise
of the most beautiful metropolis
smiling enigmatically each time
I have to justify its madness
when I find myself sketched
the perfect trace
of its finger in the sand

(Julian Semilian)

from above

if that autumn morning hadn't happened
the hot exhalations of the beheaded city
the silence fallen like a lead curtain
we still would have kept hedging our bets
on fancied battles
on imaginary geographies

the strong are lonely
the strong are sad
vulnerable in the candor
of pressing their desire so far
they can no longer follow their tracks by eye

from above it looks just the same:
the dead with the dead
the living with their vanity

(Andrei Codrescu)

the shirt of water

I inhabit a word
I moved in with my weapons, possessions and sins
ignoring my parents' advice:
don't build a house with a staircase to heaven
don't lie to yourself
when loneliness forsakes you for a brief fling
don't yearn for anyone else's illusions
and never never fall in love
with your own word, the sinful soul

the space is narrow
we can feel each other's breath—
air-vowels, earth-consonants
I pay my bills when due
and turn off the lights after every syllable

I'd consider myself a lucky tenant
except that night after night my dreams grow louder
and force me to face the unspoken
which can no longer be shut away in my shelter
then my own word occupies me like a ghost
he slips his treacherous tongue inside my unwritten pages
though enslaved, he wants me to obey only him

I live in a word as in a shirt of water
chewed-up metaphors glued to my eyelids
my master tastes his own weakness
on the tip of his tongue

(Adam J. Sorkin with Carmen Firan)

About the Authors

Nina Cassian (1924–2014), Romanian-born poet, playwright, short story writer, illustrator, composer, journalist, critic, and translator, published more than fifty books in Romania. Her major works include *La scara 1/1* (*On the Scale of 1/1* 1948), *Sufletul nostru* (*Our Soul* 1949), *An viu, noua sute si saptesprezece* (*Vital Year, 1917* 1949), *Tinerete* (*Youth* 1953), *Singele* (*Blood* 1966), *Destinele paralele* (*Parallel Destinies* 1967), *Marea conjugare* (*The Big Conjugation* 1971), *De indurare* (*Mercy* 1981), and *Numaratoarea inversa* (*Countdown* 1983). Cassian's later works include the award-winning *Call Yourself Alive?* (1988), *Life Sentence* (1990), *Cheerleader for a Funeral* (1992), and *Continuum* (2006). Sheep Meadow will publish her diaries soon.

Carmen Firan (1958-), a Romanian-born poet and fiction writer, has published twenty-five books: poetry, novels, essays and short stories. Among her recent books in the United States are *Inferno* (2010), *Rock and Dew* (2009), *Words and Flesh*, (2008), *The Second Life* (2005), *The Farce* (2003), *In the Most Beautiful Life* (2002), and several collections of poetry including *Afternoon With An Angel*, *The First Moment After Death*, and *Accomplished Error*.

Nina Cassian

Maurice Edwards anad Nina Cassian

Carmen Firan